STEELHEADING
IN
NORTH AMERICA

STEELHEADING IN NORTH AMERICA

Dave Richey

STACKPOLE BOOKS

Copyright © 1976 by
David Richey

Published by
STACKPOLE BOOKS
Cameron and Kelker Streets
P.O. Box 1831
Harrisburg, PA 17105

First printing, September 1976
Second printing (paperback) *February 1983*

Printed in the U.S.A.

Library of Congress Cataloging in Publication Data

Richey, David, 1939–
  Steelheading in North America.

  1. Steelhead fishing. 2. Fishing—North America. I. Title.
SH687.R5   799.1'7'55   776-9041
ISBN 0-8117-2149-3

To George Richey
The best of fishing companions,
and one hell of a good steelhead fisherman

OTHER BOOKS BY THE AUTHOR

TROUT FISHERMEN'S DIGEST (editor)
CHILD'S INTRODUCTION TO THE OUTDOORS
SHAKESPEARE GUIDE TO GREAT LAKES FISHING
GETTING HOOKED ON FISHING (with Jerome Knap)
SEA RUN (contributing author)

Contents

Acknowledgments

Any book requiring the research of *Steelheading in North America* could not have been written without the generous help of many people. This assistance took form in advice, photos, extended communications, personal time, etc. I am deeply indebted to the following persons and agencies: George Richey, George Yontz, Stan Lievense, Emil Dean, Paul Harvey, Richard P. Smith, David Johnson, Ludwig Frankenberger, John Scott, Jack Ellis, Peter Stricklee, Ray Gilbert, James Moore, Lee Kernen, Jim Maxwell, Gary Schnicke, Michigan Department of Natural Resources, Michigan Tourist Council, Ontario Ministry of Natural Resources, Sport Fishing Institute, U.S. Department of the Interior—Fish & Wildlife Service, Alaska Department of Fish & Game, Oregon Fish Commission, Oregon State Highway Commission, U.S. Bureau of Reclamation, Ontario Ministry of Industry & Tourism, Wisconsin Department of Natural Resources, California Department of Fish and Game, Idaho Fish & Game Department, Fisheries Division Washington Department of Game, British Columbia Fish & Wildlife Branch, Pennsylvania Fish Commission, Ohio Department of Natural Resources, Indiana Department of Natural Resources, Illinois Department of Conservation, Wisconsin Department of Natural Resources, Minnesota Department of Natural Resources, Minnesota Department of Economic Development, New York Department of Environmental Conservation, Canadian Government Office of Tourism, Eastside Boats, Marathon Rubber Products and to many other people, agencies and companies. Without their assistance, this book wouldn't have been possible.

Introduction

S teelhead fishing is many things to many people. To me it is more than a violent strike, a tug of war along a steelhead stream or the ultimate conquest of a strong, noble fish. It's more than a picture of a vanquished fish and a triumphant fisherman and definitely more than baked steelhead on the table. The real heart of steelheading is something beyond all the fishing techniques I describe in this book; it is, in fact, something difficult to put into words. It is spring months when grouse are drumming along wooded streams and early-arriving robins flit from tree to tree. It's the sight of spring steelhead digging a redd in shallow gravel and it is warm spring rains that bring fish upstream to spawn. Cloudbursts that swell rivers to overflowing are part of spring along a steelhead stream, just as much as low water along snow-covered banks when spring has forgotten to come.

Summer steelhead fishing is shirtsleeve fishing. The fish are noticeably smaller although they come to the fly hard, jump often and make an angler happy to be on the river. Summer fishing is that happy but seldom occasion when steelhead make a classic head to tail rise, suck an insect off the surface and you've remembered to carry that box of dries you so patiently tied up last winter. It makes little difference knowing that your chances of taking one of those summer fish on top is perhaps one in a million. But, when the first cast brings about a strong showy strike from a fish that surges down into your backing, doesn't that make everything all right?

Fall steelheading is a mixture of autumn wood smoke, leaves colored with Jack Frost's paintbrush, strong steelhead fresh from the sea on an early rain, and beautiful thick-sided buck steelhead that fight long and hard. Fall fishing is the savage strike of a big fish, the hard head shaking and surface gyrations, and sometimes the ultimate head toss that flips a lure or fly back into your face. You shrug your shoulders, gaze wistfully at the swirling circles where your fish disappeared, and cast again, knowing you'd be on the river during Nature's most beautiful season whether steelhead were in the river or not.

Winter steelheading is a slightly masochistic pastime. The water is cold, the air colder and the steelhead are sluggish and hard to tempt, but a steelheader knows he'd rather be on the water than home watching a football game on TV. There is something more satisfying about a solid set into a big winter fish than lolling about the house on a cold winter day. The winter fisherman must brave the worst weather nature can whip at him, but if a steelhead falls to a well-executed cast or successful drift, that angler has something that will linger in memories long after the score of the football game has dimmed.

Steelhead fishing is much more than a limit catch. It's a way of life for millions of West Coast and Great Lakes fishermen. Steelheading is a sport requiring thought, concentration, knowledge and a bit of luck to be successful. But even actually landing a big steelhead doesn't make one a complete steelhead fisherman; with a bit of luck and skill, anyone can kill a steelhead. Once you've landed the big fish that has been tearing the pool apart, worked it in close, and the fish is lying beached with its gills flaring in submission, you've won. You'll quickly admire your trophy, work the hook out and hold the fish upright in the current by its tail until it can ease off by itself. Once you've released a big steelhead into the river, that is when you become a complete steelheader.

Every fishing book reflects many purely personal opinions of its author; mine is no exception. Many fishermen may disagree with some of my opinions, but, nonetheless, this book was written with all the knowledge and humility over twenty years of steelhead fishing experience has imparted.

I'll be the first to admit that I don't know everything there is to know about steelhead fishing. In fact, I try to learn something new every time I go out. After all, fishing is a process whereby you learn by experience, and no one is an expert on any kind of fishing; some people merely know more than others.

I love steelhead fishing as much as I love life itself. If any part of this book seems self-indulgent, I hope readers will bear with my honest enthusiasm. And if in turn the reader can account for one wild leaping run or one beached steelhead as a result of reading this book, then I'll consider that I've done the job I set out to do.

Steelheading History

West Coast fishermen have pursued steelhead for sport for close to a century; for countless centuries before that, the Indians of the Northwest netted giant steelhead along coastal streams from California north to Alaska. But in fact, steelheading was a pretty limited affair until Zane Grey immortalized the species during the 1920's in his writings about the Rogue and the North Umpqua. About the same time, the advent of the automobile gave many more fishermen a chance to try for steelhead, and with its sudden popularity came many misconceptions about the life habits of steelhead. Many fishermen, for example, still contend that steelhead are a separate species of trout. Fish biologists tend to agree that the steelhead is in fact an anadromous rainbow trout; that is, a trout that migrates from fresh water to the ocean—or Great Lakes—and returns again to spawn in the stream of its birth, spending varying lengths of time in open water before going back to spawn.

Identification of a steelhead, particularly a fresh run fish or one taken from open water, is rather simple once the angler learns the various differences between similar species, like the salmon. A steelhead is similar in size and shape to both the coho and chinook salmon but small differences in body characteristics serve to distinguish them for the fisherman.

The steelhead has a typical trout-like body. The head is often smaller than salmon (more so in the case of females) although spawning males have large heads and widely-hooked jaws.

The basic open water coloration is a bright silver with dark gray to green colors on the dorsal side, fading out to a silver coloration along the lateral line. The inside of the mouth is white—a quick, easy identifying mark which differentiates a steelhead from a salmon. All Pacific salmon have a dark coloration on the inside of the mouth.

Steelhead have a generous distribution of black spots along the back and sides and these spots completely cover the dorsal fin, adipose fin and caudal (tail) fin. The black spots on the tail generally follow the rays.

The number of anal fin rays is a sure method of fish identification. Look-alike species such as steelhead, coho and chinook salmon all have different numbers of anal rays. The steelhead normally has less than twelve rays, coho have twelve to fifteen rays and the chinook salmon has fifteen to seventeen anal rays.

SPAWNING

As I have noted, the steelhead is an anadromous fish, a species that is born and lives for some length of time in fresh water, and then migrates downstream to the sea. In the case of Great Lakes steelhead, fish reared in hatcheries or in the streams migrate downstream to the vast expanses of the Great Lakes. The fish remain in the ocean or the Great Lakes until the spawning urge overtakes them; then they migrate, via a built-in homing instinct, back to their parent stream to reproduce themselves in turn.

Sexual maturation plays an important role in the coloration of the returning steelhead. Those fish that have been in the river for the largest period of time are normally also the darkest. But steelhead, especially males, often lay out in saltwater awaiting the final spawning urge and during that time body chemistry changes remove the clean silvery sheen and replace it with the darker rainbow coloration. This same chemistry is responsible for the elongation of the male fish's jaws and the formation of the "kype" or hook on the lower jaw.

While steelhead are in saltwater or the Great Lakes, the scales on the fish are rather loose, and easily knocked off by contact with rocks or other obstacles. The scales tighten after they enter freshwater.

Spawning redds are dug in pea-size gravel by the female. She arches her body and fans the gravel away with heavy lateral sweeps of her tail. The gravel drifts downstream away from the spawning bed and the tail end of the redd often looks characteristically white, due to the turning over of the gravel. The redd is often eighteen inches in diameter, three to four feet in length and as much as a foot deep. It takes a female up to six hours to complete a spawning redd although many smaller beds are dug in one to two hours' time.

Once the redd is completed the male and female enter the redd and position their vents side by side. The spawning act is accomplished by the male moving in the female's side in the shallow depression of the redd. They force their bodies down into the redd, open their mouths so that their heads are pointed slightly upward. Vigorous exertion by both fish comes to a climax as the female emits a steady stream of eggs into the gravel while the male fertilizes the eggs with cloud after cloud of milt.

A six-pound hen steelhead will carry as many as 6000 eggs; a larger ten- to fifteen-pound hen, 10,000 or more.

During the spawning process, steelhead develop pronounced spawning characteristics. Many hens will lose a portion of their bright silvery sheen and become slightly duller, similar in color to a well-tarnished but newly minted dime. Male fish often lose their silvery ocean color altogether and take on a pronounced pinkish coloration along the lateral line. The males often sport a pinkish-red gill cover, a pronounced hooked lower jaw and large canine teeth.

Great Lakes steelhead return in all sizes, shapes and—during certain times of year—different colors.

Fish from the Lake Superior area are often long, slender fish that appear very racy. These fish are always very silvery and slender in appearance. A typical Lake Superior steelhead would be twenty-six to 30 inches in length and weigh from six to ten pounds. A Lake Michigan steelhead, on the other hand, is a

Like the other salmonids, steelhead often make spectacular migratory runs and overcome great obstacles to reach their spawning waters. This steelie is headed up the Bulkey River in British Columbia. *(British Columbia Government photo)*

heavier full-bodied fish that bears little resemblance to its northern cousin. Typical steelhead from this lake often fall into two categories; the heavy pot-bellied fish (both male and female), and the slightly more slender and more streamlined fish similar to the Lake Superior steelhead. Spawning females from Lake Michigan are almost always quite silvery in appearance, while the male ranges in coloration from a vivid orangish-pink to an almost burnished black-brown fish with heavy crimson streak down its side. Heavy black dots speckle the spawning male's tail, and these dark spots are very visible in shallow water.

The thicker, heavier steelhead are often nearly as large around the midsection as they are in length. Typical pot-bellied steelhead may only be twenty-six inches in length, but scale from twelve to fourteen pounds in weight. A thirty-six-inch fish will weigh over twenty pounds. I once landed a thirteen and one-half-pound Platte River (Michigan) steelhead that was only twenty-two and one-half inches long.

Once spawning has been completed, the steelhead migrate slowly downstream toward the ocean or lake, pausing along the way to rest and to feed sporadically. Although spawning isn't supposed to be a fatal experience for steelhead, there is a heavy mortality among the older fish. The maximum life span for steelhead is approximately six years, and many steelhead spawn during their fifth or sixth year. The rigors of reproduction in advanced age is often too much for a fish to bear, and many fish succumb. Still, some steelhead, especially younger three and four-year old fish, will spawn two or three times before their life cycle ends.

When the adult fish have left the spawning area and migrated downstream, life is just beginning for the future steelhead crop. The fertilized eggs have been covered by the fanning of the female's tail buried under six to twelve inches of fine gravel.

The eggs incubate beneath this protective covering of gravel for thirty to fifty days, depending on the temperature of the water. The young steelhead evolves from an embryo into a small fry, totally dependent for a period of three or four weeks upon the egg sac. This sac soon disappears and he becomes a full-fledged steelhead fry with an unending appetite for anything smaller than he is.

Young steelhead spend up to two years of their life in the stream of their birth. During this period of time the small fish feed actively and are fed upon by larger predatory fish, birds (mainly kingfishers and herons) and man. Only the strongest steelhead fry survive this initial growing period.

Stream-raised and hatchery-grown steelhead normally grow to a length of six to ten inches before they begin feeling the urge to migrate downstream to the open water of the lake or ocean. Small steelhead are called parr before their downstream migration, and are characterized by small blotches or "parr marks" along the lateral line of the fish.

Just prior to the spring migration parr undergo a physiological change which transforms the fish into its smolt stage. This "smolting" process results in a silvery fish resembling an adult steelhead fresh in from the open water. This coloration will act as a sort of camouflage for the small trout when it reaches open water.

During their first migration, smolts slowly drift tail-first downstream on a journey that may take from just a few days to several months to complete, depending on the length of river they have to negotiate and, to a lesser extent, on their stage of development. Young smolts normally take longer to make the migration than older fish.

Once they reach open water, smolts often congregate in tidal estuaries where they feed heavily on available and abundant food: plankton, and tiny marine life, as well as minnows and crayfish. No one seems to know where steelhead migrate to once they reach open water, although many authorities feel Pacific steelhead move far off-shore and drop off the continental shelf. Great Lakes steelhead smolts have been caught many miles off shore, although some smolts do tend to hover near river mouths close to the shore.

This fly-caught steelhead exhibits the quick identifying marks which distinguish the steelhead from the salmon: the white inside of the mouth, and the black spots along the back and sides. *(Photo by the author)*

Smolting steelhead disappear for a period of two to four years before heading back to their parent streams as large, well-fed fish.

Once the spawning urge overtakes these quick-growing steelhead they begin their search for the stream of their birth. Biologists have proven that steelhead possess a highly developed olfactory sense tuned to the smell of the water from the river of their birth, and the fish use this sense of smell to home in on their spawning stream. This olfactory power is keen enough to allow the migrating steelhead to differentiate the river and the exact tributary of his upbringing. Once the steelhead moves into the river and goes through the act of reproduction, the cycle is complete and another generation of steelhead has begun.

STEELHEAD GO EAST

Basically speaking, the steelhead of West Coast streams and those of Great Lakes streams are one and the same species. All the visible characteristics of the two geographically separated fish are identical, and they react and behave in the same manner in their native waters. The only major difference between them is that the Pacific steelhead spends his time in saltwater while the Great Lakes steelhead is growing fat and sassy in a rich freshwater environment. And in fact, the Great Lakes steelhead are direct decendants of Western stock.

The story of the Great Lakes steelhead had its beginning in 1874 when rainbow trout were first brought to northeastern North America. That year one Seth Green incubated rainbow eggs at his Caledonia, New York hatchery. This original shipment of eggs was obtained from Campbell's Creek in the McCloud River system of California.

In 1876 a shipment of eggs was transferred from the McCloud River to the Northville Hatchery in Michigan. The Michigan state commission initially incubated the eggs at the Pokagon and Battle Creek Hatcheries.

Michigan's Boyne, Paw Paw and Kalamazoo rivers were stocked in 1880. Wisconsin followed Michigan's experiments in 1884, in Lake Winnebago and the Fox River. Some of these planted fingerlings soon felt the pull of open water and began a downstream migration which ultimately led them to Lake Michigan.

To accommodate this sudden interest in transplants, a steelhead egg-collecting station was operated on Redwood Creek, California between 1893 and 1898 by the U.S. Fish Commission. Stock from these California steelhead was first successfully introduced to the Great Lakes in 1895. Subsequent shipments of eggs came from the Clackamas Station, Oregon and the Puget Sound area, Columbia River and Baker Lake in Washington.

Lake Ontario was the second of the Great Lakes to be stocked with rainbow trout. Progeny from the first brood stock of the Caledonia Hatchery were planted in the headwaters of Caledonia Spring Creek and Genesee River tributaries in New York State. By 1884 some of these fish had moved downriver into the lower Genesee River and into Lake Ontario. Plantings of Canadian tributaries to Lake Ontario were first made in 1922.

Rainbow trout fry were initially planted in the Lake Erie-St. Clair River watershed (between Michigan and Ontario) during 1882. The initial plantings were made in the Clinton, Huron, and Rouge River systems and in an unnamed Ontario tributary of Lake St. Clair near Sarnia, Ontario.

Lake Huron received some of the first plantings in 1876, when the AuSable River in Michigan was stocked from the Northville Hatchery.

By 1896 the United States Fish Commission was releasing rainbows in the Tawas, Pine and Maple Rivers in Michigan. That same year the first silvery steelhead was reported from Lake Huron, a seven-pound fish taken from the Les Cheneaux Islands area in the northern part of the lake. Fish up to seven pounds were appearing regularly in the AuSable River, and between 1909 and 1913 major runs of steelhead were firmly established in the AuSable and Pine Rivers in Michigan.

Steelhead began showing up in small tributaries of the Nottawasaga River in the Georgian Bay area of Ontario in 1903. That same year showed a planting of young fish in the Sydenham River of Ontario. The first known recovery of steelhead from the Canadian waters of Lake Huron was a four pounder taken in 1904 off Manitoulin Island.

The first introduction of rainbow trout to the Lake Superior watershed was made by the Ontario Government near Sault Ste. Marie in 1883; the next planting took place in the Iron River in Michigan in 1889.

A commercially-set net harvested the first Lake Superior

steelhead in July, 1895 along the north shore. By 1897, small steelhead were being caught in Minnesota streams and in 1898, fly fishermen were having a field day in the French and Sucker Rivers near Duluth. In a two-year period at the turn of the century commercial gillnetters harvested an estimated 10,000 steelhead weighing up to eight pounds.

By the early 1920's, runs of fish were established in almost every stream at the northwestern end of Lake Superior. The eastern end of the lake likewise offered large runs of migratory rainbows.

So, from the inconspicuous beginning of a meager shipment of California rainbow eggs has come one of the most fantastic fisheries known to man. Great Lakes streams annually produce rampaging runs of steelhead, the likes of which are seldom seen except in very remote areas of the West.

Unlike their western cousins, Great Lakes steelhead have very short distances to travel to reach the upstream spawning grounds. Many eastern steelhead travel only ten to twenty miles to begin spawning while some Western fish, such as those migrating inland as far as Idaho, must overcome hundreds of miles of hazards to reach their spawning waters.

Many Midwest steelhead streams, especially those tributary to Lake Michigan, produce steelhead that average eleven pounds, and fifteen to twenty-pound fish are not uncommon. The current record steelhead from the Great Lakes is a Michigan fish that weighed twenty-six pounds, eight ounces.

The diet of Great Lakes steelhead can be described in one word: abundant. A heavy concentration of alewives provides the bulk of the steelhead's diet, and concentrated feeding efforts allow quick, heavy growth. The herring-like alewife is rich and fatty and so abundant it represents by weight over ninety percent of the fish population of the Great Lakes. With this kind of forage available, it's little wonder the steelhead of the Midwest grow to such sizes.

The small steelhead typically called "half-pounders" by westerners are seldom caught by Great Lakes fishermen. The smaller fish normally spend an extra year in the open expanses of the freshwater seas and return the following year as husky tackle-testing fish of eleven or more pounds.

In fact, there seems to be a very real difference in the ratio of weight to length between Great Lakes steelhead and those from the West Coast. On the average, Greak Lakes fish are close to

A spectacular new Eastern fishery started from hatcheries like this one in Erie county, Pennsylvania. Fishermen from Pennsylvania west to Wisconsin now enjoy the same steelheading excitement that West Coast anglers have known for close to a century. *(Penna. Fish Commission photo)*

twenty percent heavier than western fish of comparable length. Much of this difference can be directly attributed to the forage fish the two steelhead populations eat.

Western steelhead feed on forage fish less fatty than the alewife. And some biologists feel the Pacific coast fish has to work much harder to fill an empty stomach than does a steelhead from the Great Lakes.

For many years the steelhead of the Great Lakes were ravaged by the predatory sea lamprey. This villain entered the Great Lakes via the Welland Canal which was built around Niagara Falls in 1932. Sea lampreys moved inland by the millions and found fast, easy meals in the Great Lakes steelhead and lake trout.

Depredation by the lamprey—and unlimited commercial

netting—set the stage for the downfall of the Great Lakes steelhead and lake trout. Scarred and wounded steelhead were taken in spawning streams; it was evident the majestic steelhead was in serious trouble.

Then, in the 1950's an effective lampricide was discovered which began the control of lampreys in the Great Lakes. This predator is still prowling the lakes but his numbers have been rapidly reduced and, as a result, steelhead are back in numbers never before seen.

By 1966 the lamprey problem was under control, and Michigan again initiated a planting program with 182,000 steelhead fry hatched from eggs obtained from Oregon and Alaska. By 1968 and 1969, new runs of steelhead were underway, runs that staggered the imagination of the oldtime river fishermen.

Natural vs. Hatchery Fish

Steelheaders often argue the relative merits of natural versus hatchery steelhead, but there is little merit to the idea that a wild, naturally-reproduced steelhead is going to fight or taste one bit better than a hatchery reared fish. Both fish spend an equal amount of time in saltwater or in the Great Lakes before coming back to spawn.

The fighting qualities of steelhead do vary greatly from fish to fish, dependent in turn upon the water temperature, condition of the river, time of year, diet, and the individual characteristics of the fish itself. Fish of similar weight and size from the same stream often behave in drastically different ways on the end of a line. The fact that a fish was born in the stream, or spent its first year or two in a hatchery, has no bearing on the length of the battle between fisherman and steelhead.

The taste or eating qualities of a steelhead depend partially on the environment of the steelhead, the fish's diet and whether or not the fish had to migrate through pollutants which might contaminate its flesh. I'd defy anyone to judge conclusively whether a steelhead was naturally or hatchery reared by the taste test. Once the fish has attained any size it's impossible to do.

One of the real differences between Pacific coast steelhead fishing and that of the Great Lakes variety is the sheer abundance of fish in the Midwest's big lakes. A 1971 creel census in

Michigan showed nearly 600,000 steelhead taken from its streams and along its Great Lakes shoreline. This phenomenal catch record indicates a tremendous fishery success story.

Secondly, it is very rare that a steelhead is taken by an offshore fisherman in the Pacific Ocean. The only reasonably steady ocean fishery is in tidal estuaries, where steelhead often congregate before moving upstream to spawn.

Great Lakes steelhead behave in a different manner. These fish often linger for a long time in shallow lakes which form part of the tributary the fish will ascend to spawn. These small inland lakes, and to a lesser extent, the open water of the Great Lakes themselves, offer superb fishing. Fishermen knowledgeable in the ways of steelhead often find fantastic offshore fishing during certain periods of the year when steelhead hug the shorelines and rivermouths.

The Steelheader's Year

The steelhead fisherman is a fortunate individual. He has access to this king of fish during almost all periods of year. Spring, fall and winter finds steelhead in almost every stream throughout their range; summer steelhead are still looked upon by many fishermen as something of an oddity.

The angler with the means and time could travel the entire Pacific Coast, from California as far north as Alaska, and find fishing twelve months out of the year. True, not many fishermen have the time, the money or the inclination to pursue this lofty goal, but it points up the fact that, between the West Coast and the famed steelhead country of the Great Lakes, this mighty gamefish can provide a superior fishery the year around.

SPRING STEELHEADING

The months of March, April and May are the peak spring months of the migration. Actual spawning often takes place within a few days of the start of the run.

There seems to be no such creature as a spring steelhead in the Pacific Coast area; West Coast steelhead are categorized as either summer-run or winter-run fish. Actually, the Pacific winter-run steelhead do normally carry over into spring months. This is also the case in the Great Lakes area.

Great Lakes streams are much shorter than western steelhead streams. Consequently, many lake steelhead lay offshore until their eggs and milt ripen. Once the fish have reached maturation, they press upstream in heavy schools and promptly spawn.

The size of some of these spawning runs is quite unbelievable. One spring I stood knee-deep in Michigan's Little Manistee River and watched an endless procession of big steelhead moving upstream. I counted over five hundred fish the first hour. Waves of ten to twenty-pound fish just kept coming; as soon as part of a school would vacate a hole, another group would fill it, until they too moved upstream.

Pacific steelhead filter into the rivers beginning in the summer in certain areas, and the runs build up slowly during late fall, reach a peak during the winter rains, and then spawn in the headwaters during spring months. So the spawning time is basically the same even though the migration schedules often vary considerably.

That is not to say that Great Lakes steelhead do not run in the fall or early winter months—they do. The customary terminology in these two widely separated steelhead areas is slightly different. To a Great Lakes fisherman, a steelhead in the stream during springtime is a spring-run fish, pure and simple. To a West Coast fisherman, it is a winter-run fish.

Many Great Lakes fish do ascend the streams during fall and winter months and they normally winter in the rivers. The bulk of the fish are bucks; some hens make this fall or winter migration but not in nearly as high a ratio as males.

Fishing for spawning steelhead during spring months presents a very unusual set of problems. Springtime is the rainy time of year and the savvy steelheader knows which rivers are least affected by rainfall and runoff. Some streams go over their banks after a half-inch of rain; others are hardly affected by a torrential downpour. Others, their banks lined with clay, look like double-creamed coffee after a slight rainfall. Seek out streams below dams which will control flood water, rivers with lakes at the headwaters that do not drain through a swamp, or short streams with a minimum drainage system. This type of steelhead river normally isn't affected by rain and you can often find excellent fishing there while other rivers are running bank-full with runoff.

The primary thing for steelheaders to remember during the spring run is that *steelhead are not feeding.* The occasional steelhead will be found with an odd bit of food in its stomach, but these fish are *not* actively feeding. The fact that these fish aren't actively feeding doesn't mean they won't strike. Striking and feeding are two entirely different reactions.

There is some evidence to believe that steelhead begin their fast while still in the Ocean or out in the Great Lakes. This has been proven to me several times by catching a rivermouth steelhead with an empty stomach. I've gone so far as to check the stomach tract of a dozen steelhead, trying to find some trace of feeding prior to the spawning run, but so far all I've ever found is mere traces of feeding—what looked to be half-digested nymphs from a buck taken about a half-mile upstream from the estuary.

Spring Steelhead Tactics

It is essential to know where steelhead hold when they aren't up on their redds. The tail ends of drifts, deep pools, smooth runs close to shore and near any obstruction in the river are all good locations to locate resting fish.

If the spring water has warmed sufficiently to interest steelhead in spawning, the first pocket of deep water immediately upstream or downstream from a gravel bar is the best spot to look for steelies resting between bouts on the spawning bed. These deep pockets will often harbor several big fish that are using different beds in the same immediate area. The first fish caught from these pockets will often be the small, precocious male fish in the one- to three-pound size. They are impulsive strikers and will often nail a bait before their larger relatives can reach it.

I've seen resting steelhead packed into a small parcel of pocket water barely longer than they were. Six or eight fish once spooked out of a six foot pocket like this when I made a clumsy step on shore; the fish were lying within ten feet of the bank. A small pool like this one can be easily fished from shore, providing the angler doesn't spook them as I did.

Spring (or late winter on the West Coast) steelhead will be

taken most often by drift fishermen using roe or artificials. Bottom-bouncing bait or lures through deep drifts is the hottest method.

Fishing for Spawning Fish

Many streams (the headwaters at least) are closed in the West during spring months to allow the steelhead unmolested spawning. Much of the steelhead fishing Westerners enjoy is a result of natural reproduction, and the closure of these streams is a necessary thing. Great Lakes steelhead are primarily hatchery-stocked fish. Natural reproduction plays a minor role in determining the overall numbers of fish available in any given stream. Consequently many of the better spawning streams are open to fishing during the spring spawn. The headwaters of some streams (such as the Little Manistee River in Michigan) are closed until the end of April to allow the majority of the fish to spawn.

The idea of fishing for spawners rankles many western steelhead fishermen, but it's a sport sanctioned by the various Midwest states' departments of natural resources, and Midwest fishermen are accustomed to the thought of fishing for bedding steelhead. I've fished for spawning steelhead and consider it fine sport. Enough Great Lakes steelhead are planted annually to insure the runs and since a large percentage of these fish die after spawning, it seems a terrible waste of a fine gamefish not to allow fishing.

Actually, spawning fish represent one of the ultimate challenges faced by a steelhead fisherman. In areas where this sport is legal, the key to success is in being able to spot the fish before they spot you, the ability to read and judge water current, and to be able to cast accurately.

The best fishermen purposely avoid fishing for the hens. Besides the fact that there always seems to be more male fish around, if a hen is hooked, the male fish will scatter and the fisherman will lose his best opportunities to fish. For this reason, and for the reason that it is better to allow the hen to successfully spawn, only males are fished for, hooked and kept. If a hen is unavoidably hooked, the fisherman often shakes her off by giving slack line and jiggling the rodtip until the hook drops out of her mouth. They never set the hook to a hen.

Fishing for Kelts

After the spring spawn is over, surviving steelhead begin drifting downstream toward the ocean or the lakes. A brief flurry of feeding activity normally follows spawning, and deep holes will often harbor large concentrations of steelhead. The largest pools just upstream from the mouth are often some of the best spots to land kelts (spawned-out steelhead).

I've had some excellent sport catching kelts from various Western rivers. I seldom keep one of these fish for the table; they are scarred, battered, thin fish that need a couple of good months of chowing down at the big dinner table in the sea before being fit to eat. Their flesh is poor and a pale, whitish color, and lacks the flavor of a strong, robust specimen.

Kelts must be played carefully, but not to the point of exhaustion. After the rigors of spawning few fish are able to withstand the physical exertion of a long drawn-out battle. Release them gently back into the water and they might be back next year to spawn again.

SUMMER STEELHEAD

The summer steelhead is a wondrous creature; during low water periods he fills certain streams with a super-charged excitement. Small schools of steelhead move upstream from the ocean to form the advance guard of the greater fall or winter run that will follow in a matter of months.

Summer steelies are considerably smaller in size than their later-arriving cousins, but they are packed with an astounding amount of energy from head to tail. Anyone fortunate enough to tackle a summer fish on a flyrod will attest to that!

The majority of rivers noted for great steelhead fishing during winter months normally have good summer runs as well. Rivers like the Stillaguamish, Skykomish, Queets, Quinault and Kalama of Washington fame, Oregon's Rogue River or North Umpqua or California's Klamath are excellent testimonials to the fact.

"Summer run" is an all-encompassing term; actually, summer run fish, depending on location and weather, enter a river anywhere from late May through early October. The bulk of the fish *normally* make their appearnace during the months of June, July and August. Washington streams usually reach their peak

A quick dip and a four-pound summer steelhead, taken on a fly, comes to the net. (*Michigan Tourist Council photo*)

during July. British Columbia streams often peak during August, while summer runs in Oregon and California usually peak during July and August.

Although Washington probably has the locks on summer steelheading in the continental United States (at least as far as numbers of streams go), British Columbia stands head and shoulders above any other area for sheer numbers of summer-run steelhead streams.

British Columbia has a veritable smorgasbord of summer-run streams on the west coast of Vancouver Island as well as all along the mainland. Summer steelhead ascend many of the known and recorded streams on Vancouver Island and the mainland as well as many more northerly mainland streams that currently are going unfished.

Fish ascending these streams usually weigh from four to ten pounds during summer months, although a ten-pounder is considered by many experts a large summer fish. The average size is somewhere between four and eight pounds.

And the Pacific slope isn't the only area that has a summer steelhead fishery. Michigan's Sturgeon River, in the Lower Peninsula, has the only confirmed Midwest run of summer fish. This river flows into Burt Lake, a large relatively shallow body of water that warms considerably during a hot summer. Steelhead in the lake migrate up the Sturgeon River once the lake water becomes uncomfortable—usually around the first of July. Steelhead remain in the river through the fall months, and some fish winter over to spawn in the spring.

Some fishermen maintain this "temperature run" isn't a true summer steelhead run, but the fish are there, and it's hard to argue with good steelheading in the summer months.

The Betsie River, which flows into Lake Michigan, is another Michigan stream that hosts the odd summer steelhead. Some fish are caught during June through August although not in sufficient numbers to be classified as a true run.

What is it that makes the summer steelhead so special? Many things. First of all, summer steelhead migrate upstream at a time of year when there is very little else to consider in the way of good fishing action. Secondly, the fish are of fair size, full of fight and are capable of taking an angler down into his backing in just a few seconds of headlong flight.

The one factor that endears summer fish to the hearts of steelhead fishermen is their willingness to take a fly. In summer the rivers are at their lowest points, and fish are concentrated in deeper water. Once he locates a feeding school, the cautious fisherman can have a field day with high-jumping summer steelhead. With low water conditions prevailing, the angler has wide gravel bars from which to cast and do battle. These broad bars enable the flyfisherman to make long easy backcasts without fear of fouling his line in trees and bushes behind him.

Summer Steelhead Tactics

Shallow stretches, where bottom boulders can be easily seen, are usually not frequented by summer fish. The summer fisherman should figure on fishing some of the deepest water he can find. I've found summer steelhead prefer holes eight or more feet deep. If water of this depth isn't available, search out the deepest drifts and concentrate your fishing efforts there.

Summer steelhead also seek out heavy flows of current for safety. The head of a pool, just downstream from a whitewater riffle, is often a good spot to try. These areas are highly oxygenated and, perhaps as a result, the fish seem to fight harder.

Deep holes normally found beneath road bridges are often hotspots for summer fish because they provide cool, deep water and the relative safety of darkness. I've taken many summer steelhead from beneath highway bridges. These pools are often fished heavily during the day, and I've had my best success by either being the first person under the bridge at daybreak or by sticking with it until other fishermen leave just before dark. In fact, early and late hours of low light intensity are usually the best hours for summer steelheading. Many times the fish will be found in shallow lies during these periods, before they drift into deeper water during midday.

Summer steelhead are finicky creatures; they'll often chase a lure or fly clear across a stream without striking, a habit which can be unnerving to a beginning steelheader. Veteran fishermen often solve this problem by presenting either a larger or smaller lure or fly, or one of a totally different color; very often the next cast will result in a jarring strike. Many steelheaders make about fifteen casts with one fly or lure and then change. They feel a summer fish should have struck by then if he was interested in the offering.

These summer fish are unusually aggressive strikers and a competitive spirit prevails among school fish to see which one will be first to grab a fly or lure. I've taken as many as six steelies from one school in a tiny pocket of deep water in less than a half-hour. On every cast I could watch a half-dozen fish compete for my spinner. I released all but one seven-pounder that day, but I had thrilled to a dozen strikes on fifteen casts. That kind of summer action is enough to hook any fisherman on steelheading.

Part of the key to successful summer steelheading is covering lots of water. It is imperative to fish an area quickly but thoroughly and then move on if contact with fish hasn't been made. Many days I've covered five miles before I've found a school of summer fish.

I've found the best method is to fish a small area for no longer than fifteen minutes. I'll spend up to a half hour on the larger drifts. If you don't have a strike in ten or fifteen minutes then it's logical to assume there are no fish available. Pack up and move on to the next likely-looking area.

Another key to successful summer fishing is a careful approach to drifts and riffles once fish are located. Noise will spook a steelhead or school of fish in short order. Move slowly, step carefully, wade silently and keep rod movement to a minimum.

Spinning

In summer, steelhead take lures readily—small Mepps spinners, Okie Drifters, spawn bags and other typical steelhead lures. Although the fish will chase a fly, it is considered best to fish lures in the conventional manner along bottom (bottom fishing with bait and lures will be covered in a following chapter).

A hot summer fishing technique I've used with spinning gear involves the use of light line—4 to 6 pound test. A small snap swivel and a tiny silver Mepps spinner in size 1 or 2 completes the rig. In fast water I add one or two tiny split shot for weight.

I wade slowly and softly downstream, with frequent stops. Summer fish often lie tight along submerged tree trunks or near brush piles and boulders. This type of cover offers both shade and safety.

The object is to cast quartering across and downstream and sweep the spinner over the tops of logs, boulders and other deepwater hiding spots. A rambunctious summer fish will chase the spinner almost every time it passes over his lie. I've used this method to locate schools of summer steelhead on many rivers.

One time I was working the cedar-lined banks of the Sturgeon River in Michigan. It was late in July and a large school of steelhead had been seen moving out of Burt Lake the day before. I figured their overnight travel would take them a couple miles upstream.

The next morning I started my search under a bridge about

three miles upstream from the lake. A dozen casts in the deep hole beneath the bridge produced nothing but a half-hearted follow from a resident brown of about sixteen inches.

I hopscotched downstream, concentrating my attentions on likely-looking spots. A summer steelhead boiled out from beneath a submerged stump and hammered my spinner. I pounded the hooks home and held on as six pounds of infuriated steelhead cartwheeled across the surface and then lit out on a mad dash downstream. I stumbled along through thigh-deep water in an attempt to keep up. Fifteen minutes later and two hundred yards downstream I slid the exhausted male onto a grassy beach, gently worked out the spinner hook and held him upright in the water until he swam off under his own power.

I moved back upstream and slowly and methodically worked the pocket of water along both sides and behind the stump. One other small half-pounder slammed the spinner but I missed the strike. I worked the area for fifteen minutes and then continued my search downstream.

A mile of river washed past my waders before I found a school of about twenty fish laying in a deep pocket behind a birch tree that had toppled into the river. They were partially hid among logs and rocks in six feet of water. If it hadn't been for the sunlight glinting off the sides of a fish as it chased a small stream trout I wouldn't have spotted him.

I made my first cast and three fish rose smoothly off bottom and raced each other to the spinner. The twinkling blade flopped once as a fish struck and missed and the other fish peeled over like fighter pilots and headed for bottom.

Two more casts to the same area failed to produce a strike although I could still see the fish and knew they weren't spooked. I quickly took off the silver spinner and replaced it with a smaller sized copper model. A four-pound fish jetted up off bottom as the spinner swung over its head and nailed the spinner hard.

The hook was set on the strike and this fish churned the river apart as he did a nonstop series of headshaking pinwheels across the water. Five jumps later the drag was whining as the fish raced downstream toward Burt Lake. Ten minutes later my second fish of the day was beached and released.

I stuck with that school for several hours and wound up landing a total of five fish, although I hooked and lost several other fish on jumps or to line-grabbing debris. I kept one deeply hooked four-pounder for the table and released the others un-hurt.

Summer steelhead are like that; find a school of active fish and the fisherman can usually stick with it for several hours or until the fish decide to move upstream.

If strikes are coming on a steady basis, and then suddenly stop for no apparent reason, chances are good the fish have left that particular hold and have migrated further upstream. The trick here is to move upstream until you come to another likely looking area and try it. Keep moving and trying new spots until the fish are located again.

There are times when summer steelhead will reveal their presence by rolling or splashing on the surface. Many anglers just walk the banks and watch the river for surface disturbance to reveal the whereabouts of fish. This rolling and splashing takes place usually early in the morning and again just before dark.

Fly Fishing For Summer Steelhead

Summer steelhead, due to their increased time in freshwater, are much more prone to feed actively. This is the predominant reason why summer fish rise so well to a well-presented fly.

The majority of flyfishermen cast quartering across and downstream and allow the fly to swing around on a tight line. The fly can be given some action with a slow hand twist retrieve or by jiggling the rodtip. I've had success using both methods.

Another method of presenting the fly is to cast quartering across and downstream and mend the line by rolling a small loop of line upstream. This eliminates drag by reducing the belly in the line and its resistance to water. The majority of steelhead will strike as the fly begins to swing around in the current on a tight line. The swinging action causes the fly to swim toward the surface, and steelhead will lift off the bottom to intercept it.

Many times summer steelhead will take a streamer or wet fly just under the surface. There are times when a weighted fly is needed to provoke a strike from inactive fish. The wise steelheader will carry an assortment of flies in all sizes, colors, and to a lesser degree, patterns. Hook size and color are often more important factors in producing strikes than is a change in fly pattern.

There are certain instances when summer steelhead will rise and take dry flies off the surface. These happy occasions are indeed rare, but the fisherman should be prepared to offer the steelhead a drag-free float of a dry fly if the conditions warrant. A floating flyline takes up very little space in the fishing vest.

Summer steelhead are grand fish to hook into, whether you are fishing one of the large West Coast rivers or a small intimate stream like the Sturgeon in Michigan. A summer-run fish will make an excellent showing on light tackle, and anyone that has experienced the heart-pounding thrill of a dancing summer steelhead will come back for more.

FALL STEELHEADING

The fall steelhead is a magnificent, finely-tuned fighting machine dressed in a battle suit of chrome silver. He's headstrong, hard to hold when hooked and jumps like something possessed. There's nothing quite as determined and difficult to control as a fresh-hooked fall steelhead.

Great Lakes fishermen are used to having steelhead appear in their streams during the October through December period; hence, the term fall steelhead applies. West Coast fishermen categorize their fish differently. A steelhead entering freshwater in October could be a late-running summer fish or an early-running winter fish. Few anglers along the Pacific shoreline classify their steelhead runs as being fall-run. In fact, almost every western river having a decent run of summer steelhead will have a carryover run of fish during the fall and early winter months. But the fall-running fish in these rivers are traditionally much larger.

Along the Pacific slope fall steelhead runs are dependent upon rainfall to open the tidal bars at the river mouth. If rains do not come in significant amounts until late in the year, which often happens, steelhead that could ascend the river have to wait until winter. There are odd years when rains come early and steelhead are in the rivers during the actual fall months. Great Lakes rivers have free and open access to the open water of the Great Lakes and steelhead runs are often in full swing during the gorgeous full color months of late September, October and early November.

Canadian rivers along the Lake Superior shoreline often have a peak migration period in approximately mid-October. Minnesota's North Shore streams peak about the same time. Lake Huron and Michigan streams peak out during November or early December.

Fall Steelheading In The Great Lakes

Fall steelhead fishermen find some fantastic fishing along the Great Lakes shorelines anytime after Labor Day. Cooler weather and the cooling off of the lake water will bring steelhead close to the beaches. Fishermen home in on rivermouths and secluded beaches for a try at this tremendous gamefish in the surf.

This type of open water fishery doesn't seem to excite West

Fall weather brings the Great Lakes steelhead closer to shore, where the angler can try for big fish in the surf. *(Photo by the author)*

Coast fishermen. Altogether too many sportsmen just bide their time and wait for the rains to open the tidal bars when they could be experimenting and trying for openwater steelhead in the Pacific.

I'll grant that many areas of the Pacific shoreline are just too rugged for surf fishing and it's also true that the vast expanse of water is difficult to strain in search of a cruising steelhead. But, as years go by and more people are drawn into steelheading, someone will come up with the answer on how to catch steelhead with some consistency from the Pacific Ocean. It can be done. Of that I'm sure. It's a matter of how, when and where.

Some West Coast streams such as Klamath, Rogue, North Fork of the Umpqua and the Kispiox all have what could be loosely classified as fall runs of steelhead. The peak in these rivers often comes from mid-September through mid-October. Weather conditions have a great deal to do with fall steelhead runs in these rivers.

The last two or three years have shown a tremendous buildup of fall-spawning steelhead in several Michigan and Wisconsin streams. Nit-pickers would call these fall spawners large domesticated strains of Wisconsin rainbows. Steelhead fishermen call them steelhead.

These steelhead are hefty fish, wide of girth and short in length. The males ascend the rivers in full spawning colors with vivid reddish-orange sides and reddish-pink gill covers. Large hooked jaws are present in sexually mature males. Females spawning during the October to December period arrive in the rivers, often after the first heavy fall rains, in a sexually mature state.

The fall spawners often mix right in with spawning coho and chinook salmon. I've seen a tendency, over the last three years, for fall spawning steelhead to make their redds closer to the lake than spring fish. Many times they'll spawn within a few miles of Lake Michigan or Huron. A few fall-spawning steelhead have shown up in Lake Superior streams although this strain of fish is not prevalent there.

The exciting thing about fall-spawning fish is the fact they make a valuable contribution to the fall fishery. And they are big fish.

I was fishing Michigan's Big Manistee River, with a customer aboard my river boat, when my client had a jarring strike on a Flatfish. Fifty yards downstream a great thick fish arched into the air, splashed back and jetted off downstream.

I quickly worked up the anchor and we drifted downstream. The massive steelhead vaulted into the air again next to the boat and turned upstream. Twisting head shakes and violent body contortions rippled up the line, through the rod and down my customer's arm. The male slashed up out of the water and I could hear my customer audibly gulp at the apparent size of the fish. "He's twenty pounds," my man was stammering.

The fish fought the current and rod pressure and finally uncorked one last feeble jump as he drifted downstream and I worked the net under the tired old fish. As I lifted him into the boat I marveled at the girth of the fish—but he felt pretty light in the net. It was a big fish but no twenty-pounder.

I took a few pictures of my customer and his big fall-spawning male and then we taped him. The slab sided fish was 23 inches in length, had a tail about ten inches wide and weighed just a couple ounces shy of fourteen pounds. It was the largest trout for its length I've ever seen caught.

I've caught many males dressed up in their orange-pineapple colored spawning clothes since then, and the striking thing about these fish is their sheer beauty. Some fishermen call them "footballs" in a derogatory manner because of their length-girth ratio, but I find fall spawning males extremely handsome and strong fighters.

Females spawning in the fall seldom tarry long in one spot, but arrive fresh from the Great Lakes in a silvery coat and they hurry directly to the spawning grounds. I've watched a fall spawning pair of fish completely spawn out within one day. Fish like this often survive to spawn again because the rigors of upstream travel and spawning chores don't sap their strength as much as a long upstream migration for hundreds of miles does.

Many fall run steelhead are not going to spawn for several weeks—or for as long as four to five months. The fish swarm up the rivers in loose schools from a half-dozen to as many as one hundred fish at a time. They will press upstream for a short period and then pause for varying lengths of time in pools and runs. Fall fish often hold in one general area for two or three days and up to a week before moving on. Many times the urge to travel further upstream is coupled with a heavy rainstorm.

The average fall-running fish takes its time, but they relentlessly push upstream toward the spring spawning water. Many fall steelhead will find a hole or run to their liking and spend a great deal of time in it once they reach striking distance of the headwaters. I've found that large deep pools or hydro dams will often hold pre-spawning steelhead for long periods of time, often until the reproductive urge becomes strong early in the spring.

In Michigan I've noticed that steelhead migrating upstream during fall months tend to be largely male fish. Of course, many females with strings of roe about as big around as a small cigar and the eggs still sticking tightly to the membrane are caught, but a disproportionate number of the fish taken will be bucks. In turn, the biggest push of Great Lakes steelheads comes during March and April and a large percentage of this run will be females ready to spawn seeking bedding sites and ready males.

I've talked with many western anglers and found that many of their shorter rivers have the same phenomenon. The simple explanation is that many female steelhead simply wait until just prior to spawning before they ascend the river. Of course, there are many exceptional cases of hens pushing upstream during fall months, wintering in deep holes and spawning in the spring.

The fall steelheader has possibly the best season of the year in which to practice his sport. The weather is often balmy, the soft breezes drifting through the golden crowns of hardwood-lined streams in the Midwest, through the majestic redwoods of the Northwest, or along a secluded stream in primitive sections of Ontario or British Columbia.

The water levels are low and clear and the first hint of approaching winter may come with a touch of frost early in the morning. Steelhead are invigorated by the cooling water and a freshly hooked fish is a sight to behold. Hard-to-handle rocketing downstream dashes are usually accompanied by a series of head-shaking leaps that often leave the angler with a limp line and an incredulous look as he asks his partner, "Did you see that?"

Even at moments like this, a true angler will admit fall steelhead fishing is one of the most productive times of year—as well as being the most beautiful season for a steelheader to be on the water.

Winter flyfishing for steelhead is cold business in the Midwest, but the big winter fish bring out the best in the anglers who're willing to try for them. *(Michigan Tourist Council photo)*

Winter Steelheading

Winter steelhead fishing is a state of mind, as well as a statement of the prevailing weather conditions. West Coast steelhead fishermen firmly believe the winter run isn't on, or won't be on, until heavy winter rains swell the rivers, wash out tidal sandbars and fill the steelhead with an urgency to move upstream. Once the first rains of winter arrive, steelheaders from California to British Columbia hasten to their favorite rivers. Ears are glued to radio or television weather forecasts as fishermen second guess the rains in an effort to determine which rivers are fishable and which will be over their banks. Phone calls are made, reservations at motels are booked and the steelhead fisherman begins his cold and lonely duel with winter fish.

The Great Lakes fisherman is also a winter steelheader although his fishing may be more wintry, in the classic sense of the word, than his West Coast buddy's. Our Midwest friend suffers snowstorms, icy blasts that freeze guides and fingers, floating chunks of ice in some rivers, impassable backroads and a chill factor that would make most fishermen wonder why they ever started steelhead fishing in the first place.

Winter steelheading in both areas is a cold, demanding sport that places the highest emphasis on physical stamina, concentration, and angling ability.

Steelhead begin running as early as October or November in the Great Lakes and as late as December and January in the Northwest, where the peak of the run is usually determined entirely by rainfall. Early rains will bring fish in during the late fall while a late rainy season will hold Pacific steelhead in the ocean until after the first of the year.

Great Lakes winter runs are basically an overlapping of the fall run, which usually begins in October. Fish keep coming throughout the winter, although the runs slow down considerably during January and February due to the extremely cold water conditions. The fall-winter run then builds to a peak during the spring migration in March and April.

A certain amount of overlapping occurs on West Coast rivers, although winter runs are much more distinct and winter months are a prime fishing period for anglers.

River volume of Great Lakes streams varies little from season to season, although water downstream near the mouth will be completely covered with a solid mantle of ice once winter locks in. The only hazard of winter steelhead fishing in the Great Lakes is unseasonably warm weather or rain, which melt the snow cover and put the streams over their banks. January or February thaws can make the rivers almost unfishable.

West Coast streams are also subject to the effects of the weather pattern. Wet years, with average or above-average amounts of rainfall, mean the rivers are high and steelhead are free to press upstream without restriction. During wet years West Coast steelheaders find their best fishing near the headwaters or in smaller creeks and streams tributary to the main river. Dry years on the coast create a totally different set of circumstances. The Western angler must concentrate on the larger streams, whose increased flow of water will allow some fish to pass. And during low-water dry years, he must fish nearer the mouth of the river. Steelhead will often be found in the lower stretches of a stream.

Winter Tactics

Winter steelheading is known more for its challenge than for its productivity. Still, it is almost always possible to catch some winter steelhead, providing you have more than one day to fish. Winter conditions place a heavy demand on the angler to be flexible and swing with the moods of the rivers. Some winter steelheaders drive as much as 300 miles to change locations.

A point to keep in mind about winter fishing: rivers containing one or two dams upstream from the Pacific or Great Lakes have a more stable water temperature and water flow than rivers unimpeded by a dam. The hydro dam will stabilize the water flow and steelhead find a steady flow of water to their liking. A river without a dam may have a fluctuating water level due to rainfall, snow melt, or runoff from tributaries. Any or all factors can greatly affect your chances of success.

Water temperature is an important factor in winter fishing. Water temperatures often dip as low as 34° F and fish are downright sluggish in water that cold. The best fishing occurs when the water temperature is 45° F or slightly warmer. In the Great Lakes peak winter runs often occur just as winter's ice pack drops away from inland lakes upstream from the mouth. Steelhead seem to sense the break-up of the ice, and ascend the rivers in heavy schools.

Stream fishing techniques vary only slightly from spring or fall methods. There are a few tricks that pertain more to winter fishing than any other season of the year.

Since the water temperature is cold, and the steelhead are rather sluggish, it pays to fish right down on bottom with any bait or lure. The fish will have his head buried in the gravel and it takes something bouncing off his nose to bring off a strike.

Fish each drift slowly and thoroughly. A drift you could fish through quickly in warmer weather demands more attention during winter's cold spells. If you feel a steelhead is holding in a certain lie, slow your fishing pace down to a crawl and give the fish a second or third chance at your bait; sometimes that will be the key between hooking a fish or missing out on a strike.

Cold-weather steelhead strike less readily than at other times of the year. They tend to mouth a bait or merely peck at a swinging lure; repeated casting often gives the fish another chance.

Many feeder streams and tributaries of larger rivers host runs of steelhead in the spring. And many times winter fish will lie just upstream or downstream from a smaller stream and wait until the water conditions are favorable to enter and spawn. Fish just above and below an inflowing stream during winter months. These places are often very productive for a month or so immediately prior to the normal spawning period.

Some of the finest steelhead fishing I've ever witnessed came during winter rainstorms or snowstorms. Falling rain or snow is usually warmer than the river water and this often triggers a favorable reaction from fish.

Bright sunny winter days also bring about good steelhead fishing, particularly if they follow a two- or three-day low pressure center or a storm. I've known many occasions on dark overcast days when it seemed almost impossible to get a strike. Suddenly the sun would peek through the cloud cover for several minutes and someone would hook a fish. Two or three strikes later the sun disappeared again—and so did the fish. On winter days, get your licks in while the sun is shining. A two or three day stretch of spring-like weather is an excellent time to go fishing. The warmth of the sun, the resulting snow melt, and slightly warmer water temperatures often put fish on the prod.

Great Lakes winter fishermen must also contend with ice conditions. Once, my brother had his heart set on fishing Lake Michigan off the Wisconsin shoreline, but the prevailing wind kept ice floes pushed against the beach. When a turn-around of the wind pushed the ice back into Lake Michigan, he hurried to the beaches and caught several fish by wading out and casting bait and small spoons.

Ice Fishing For Steelhead

Some Midwest anglers have recently discovered ice fishing for steelhead; this approach had never been tried before. Prime locations are inland lakes or bays where steelhead must pass through on their way upstream. The focal points are the mouths of rivers entering into the lakes. Lake ice off a rivermouth can be very unstable, even dangerous; caution is required in fishing a lake where flowing water is nearby.

I use a Jiffy Power Ice auger to drill several widely spaced holes, trying different areas until I find an area the steelhead are using.

A short open-face spinning rod and reel is the best tackle. Most of the steelhead are taken with small jigs or spoons such as a Swedish Pimple, S'Vede, Lujon, Eppinger Devele Dog, Barracuda jig or jigging Rapala.

A winter steelheader in the Great Lakes can also go after fish through the ice. *(Photo by the author)*

Stand back from the ice hole and lower the lure near bottom and begin jigging up and down with short strokes. Pause at the end of each jigging movement. If nothing happens near bottom, move the lure upward a foot or two and try again. Sooner or later you'll be rewarded with a savage strike and a new kind of battle as you try to control a fish under the ice. The drag on your reel has to be set properly (less than one half of the breaking strength of the line) or the fish will be on its way with a lure stuck in his lip, and all you'll have is a broken line. Jagged ice at the bottom of the hole will cut the line if you aren't careful.

Landing an ice-bound steelhead takes a bit of doing. The best bet is to be sure the trout is thoroughly tired out before leading it to the hole. Time the steelhead's arrival at the hole so the fish comes in head first. Get his head started and skim him swiftly out onto the ice.

Winter steelhead fishing is a cold, rugged sport that demands the utmost in fishing skill. The rewards are meager in terms of numbers of fish landed (West Coast fishermen generally land more winter steelhead than Great Lakes fishermen partially because they enjoy slightly warmer weather conditions along the Pacific Ocean). But steelhead fishing wouldn't be steelhead fishing if an angler didn't have to put up with snow, rain and cold weather. Some wag once said, "A steelhead fisherman has to suffer". If that is the case, I've paid my dues, and it's all been worth it.

Steelhead Tackle and Accessories

As in any other type of fishing, the proper selection of equipment is paramount to steelhead success. Steelhead *can* be hooked and landed with non-descript rods, reels and terminal tackle but a wise choice of equipment will make it all a much easier and more enjoyable experience.

Let's take a look at the different types of rods, reels and other tackle needed for steelhead fishing. I'd like to point out here that there is no such thing as a perfect steelhead outfit; the important point to remember is the fisherman must outfit himself for the "type" of fishing he'll encounter. It takes a specialized piece of equipment to fish brushy streams just as it takes a powerful flyrod to belt out one hundred-foot casts into the teeth of a winter gale blowing in off the Pacific. No single rod and reel combination can meet all the demands of steelheading. The solution, for the majority of steelhead fishermen, is the acquisition of several steelhead outfits, each geared to a specific job on a specific type of water.

RODS

A wise choice of rod—baitcasting, flyrod or spinning—is important to the steelheader. The proper selection of rod will enable the fisherman to cope with long runs and sudden powerful struggles close to the net. A good rod will help make the landing of a big steelhead an easier job.

The proper steelhead rod doesn't vary much in length from West Coast streams to the Great Lakes; the average rod, regardless of type, is 8 to 9 feet long. It is possible to use a shorter rod for some types of fishing, but the 9-foot stick allows the fisherman to cover the water much better than a shorter rod. A longer rod also aids in the final playing and landing of a big steelhead.

Small bushy rivers can be adequately covered with a 7½ to 8-foot rod. And smaller rods have a distinct advantage when negotiating stretches of brush to get to the river.

The bulk of today's steelhead rods are manufactured from fiberglass under a variety of different processes. Each manufacturer has his own process of rod building and it should be enough to just state that when buying rods, buy quality and brand names. Steer clear of department store specials and "cheapies."

Some fishermen believe the color of a rod has a bearing on their fishing. I've personally used white Shakespeare rods for many years and in my experience, rod color does not affect the fish.

Several rod manufacturers are now building rods from carbon filament materials, or graphite, marketed under various brandnames such as Graflite and others. These rods are light, weighing an average of less than two ounces. Now being manufactured in spinning, fly and baitcasting models, this type of rod is exceptionally strong for its weight; stronger than a comparable rod made from glass. Carbon filament (graphite) construction results in faster rod recovery with less vibration, which transfers a higher degree of sensitivity through the rod and into the hands of the angler. In other words, fast recovery and lack of vibration allows the fisherman to react quicker to the strike.

Guides are extremely important on a steelhead rod because they spread the line load evenly along the entire rod. Generally speaking, the more guides on a rod the better it will perform. Both spinning and baitcasting rods are being built with glass ferrules, which tend to spread the stress evenly throughout the entire length of the rod. A locking reel seat is a must for every kind of rod.

Spinning Rods

Of the thousands of anglers that fish steelhead each year, I'd wager the largest percentage of them fish with spinning outfits—not the cheaper spin-cast rigs, but good well-made spinning rods produced by reputable companies.

The average 8½ to 9-foot spinning rod is a fairly stiff stick, with a powerful butt section for setting the hook and a rather limber tip section, the better for keeping the feel of bait or a lure drifting through a pool. A good rod will have evenly spaced rod guides, with a larger gathering or stripper guide at the bottom and a carboloy tiptop guide. Two-piece rods are best. Single piece rods are an abomination to carry and transport.

Flyrods

Flyrods are a completely different story. Here again the importance of knowing the type of water you'll be fishing figures in determining of the type of rod you'll need. Flyrods for steelhead fishing come in sizes rated from a number 6 (which would be an excellent choice for small streams and summer steelhead) up to the heavy number 10 and 11 rods. The latter rods are used for big rivers where wind and long distance casting are constant factors. Most rivers of moderate size can be fished with an 8 or 9 line.

Steelhead fly fishing often calls for casts of sixty to eighty feet, and some rivers always offer the best lies ninety to one hundred ten feet away—on the opposite side of the river. Your flyrod must have the guts to handle long lengths of line in an effortless manner.

Shorter flyrods also hamper roll casting so that the fisherman often must wade into different positions when a simple roll cast would present the fly properly. Good grade flyrods and by a brand name manufacturer should have a controlled flexing action that will bend all the way from the tip to the butt section without any flat spots. Most of our modern flyrods bear the weight number on the butt section of the rod just ahead of the cork grip. This serves to aid the fisherman in selecting a rod and line that will balance each other.

Good fiberglass flyrods can be had for twenty-five to fifty dollars.

Bamboo flyrods have a definite cult following among fishermen, but few steelheaders care to take a favorite bamboo stick on the river for a day of steelhead fishing. Bamboo rods are more subject to having a "set" form in their tip section and older bamboo rods have a bad habit of bursting apart under the stresses placed on them by the savage steelhead. A good bamboo rod will cost upwards of one hundred dollars, after all.

The newer carbon filament flyrods are receiving widespread attention from flyfishing steelheaders. The rods are tough, light enough for all-day effortless casting but, as of this writing, they are still quite expensive, although improved production costs and competition will undoubtedly force the price to a more reasonable level.

Trolling Rods

Trolling rods can be jury-rigged from any type of spinning or baitcasting rod, but the best trolling rods are coupled with level wind baitcasting reels in the 7½- to 8-foot range. Trolling rods should be sturdy enough in the butt section to help anchor the hook when a steelhead strikes on a long line, but still soft enough in the tip to telegraph the lure action. Trollers often pick up fallen leaves and other debris on their lures and the rodtip should be sensitive enough to allow the alert angler to detect the difference in the action of his lure. Most spinning, baitcasting or trolling rods can be purchased for under thirty dollars.

There are some speciality rods for steelhead fishing, constructed to meet a demanding type of fishing. An example would be an 11-foot soft-action single-egg spinning rod; these rods are often custom built to suit a particular angler's needs. Single-egg rods are made especially soft for lob casts and to help absorb the shocks of steelhead fishing with a light line. A conventional rod doesn't have the necessary give to provide the angler with the extra cushion needed when fishing with a 2-, 4- or 6-pound monofilament.

REELS
Spinning Reels

Spinning reels have probably done more to make steelhead fishing the popular pastime it is today than any other piece of equipment. Spinning reels have made it very easy for new fishermen to cast accurately and with good distance—two requirements for consistent productivity on a steelhead stream.

With a rod and line to match, a spinning reel allows the angler to cast lures from one-eighth ounce up to one ounce or more, with little loss in accuracy or fish-catching ability.

A good spinning reel will be a medium-size open face model with a full bail. Shakespeare, Garcia, Heddon, Quick and others make fine quality spinning reels suitable for use on steelhead. You need neither the ultra-light nor the light saltwater models. The Shakespeare 2062 or the Mitchell 300 is a good example of the type and size to buy.

A smooth non-stick drag is of prime importance for spinning. The best drags usually have six discs of leather, rubber, asbestos, cork or other material. The discs work against each other to increase or reduce friction. Normally a screw-down device is used to increase the friction by compressing the discs against each other. Many veteran steelheaders go their store-bought drags one better and lubricate the discs with Never Seez compound which will smooth out any drag. The key to any good drag is to keep it free of dirt and grime.

Quality spinning reels have an anti-reverse lever which I always leave on the "on" position. I've known big steelhead to surprise a fisherman with a violent strike or sudden change of direction that can pull the reel handle out of his hands. If the anti-reverse lever isn't on, the reel handle spins backwards out of control, the fish gets slack line and is gone before the fisherman can recover.

When buying a spinning reel check to see if the roller on the bail revolves under line pressure. The roller assures even distribution of line from the reel to the rod guides; if it isn't working, it can become grooved from constant line wear and cut your line when you hook a big fish.

Baitcasting Reels

Baitcasting reels are a pure joy to fish with, providing you've educated your thumb and can cast without suffering a backlash

These hefty California steelhead were taken on a baitcasting rig with a HotShot lure. *(Photo by Jack Ellis)*

every time. The pinpoint accuracy that can be obtained with a baitcasting rig cannot be equalled even with a spinning outfit.

A baitcasting reel should be of the smaller sizes such as Shakespeare's 1975 or Ambassedeur's 5000 reel. Ball bearing type reels are good, but not really worth the extra money. Insist on buying a baitcasting reel with a level wind device and a centrifugal drag system, so that you can adjust the reel to compensate for casting weights of almost any size.

The better baitcasting reels have a star drag system built into the reel smooth enough to cope with the lightning charge of an infuriated steelhead. This star drag is right at hand and easily adjustable during the course of a fight.

The baitcasting arbor should be constructed of a material that will not split and break under the heavy pressure of compressed monofilament line. Old reels will often burst apart when subjected to the brutal pressure of tightly spooled mono.

Fly Reels

Fly reels are relatively easy to choose because their main purpose is to store line. Steelhead fishermen often play their fish directly off the reel, which is the recommended procedure when fighting a powerful fish. A fly reel selected for steelhead fishing should be large enough to hold at least one hundred yards of monofilament or braided Dacron backing and the flyline. Many companies offer single action fly reels in a variety of sizes to handle different size lines and rods.

Look for a strong, one-piece frame that is both lightweight and strongly constructed. All steelhead flyreels should be bought with the idea of adding extra spools at a later date. Many anglers like to carry floating, sinking, wet tip and other type of flylines to match river conditions.

Single action fly reels will have a sturdy reliable drag that is positive when a fish takes line, but will not create a drag when line is being reeled in. Martin Reel Company manufactures a well-made single action reel with multiplying retrieve. This reel operates at about a four to one ratio on the retrieve, which comes in handy when a steelhead turns and runs back upstream. I've had it happen, and believe me, it's impossible to strip or reel line fast enough to stay tight to a hard-swimming steelhead when he makes up his mind to head upstream.

The automatic reel serves as a quick and convenient means of bringing in slack line. For the most part, automatics do not serve the steelhead fisherman adequately. Automatic flyreels are used to a very small extent in some Great Lakes states, where the angler stocks the reel with 30 pound mono and man-handles the fish in shallow brushy water. The fish is hooked and fought on a short line and not allowed to run.

Fly reels range in price from about $25 to over 100, depending on the size and make reel you desire. Quality American-made reels that perform just as well as higher-priced reels imported from Europe can be purchased for about thirty dollars.

LINES

Monofilament

Monofilament can be the cheapest and yet the most expensive piece of equipment you purchase. Monofilament is cheap only if you buy the best line you can afford and change it often. If you neglect your mono, store it in the sun or a warm place, and then hook a big steelie only to see your line part with a sound like a pistol shot, you'll quickly see how expensive line can be.

Tremendous advancements have been made in the production of monofilament in recent years. Today's mono has gotten smaller in diameter, has higher knot strength, and is slightly more resistant to heat and sunlight.

The best advice for beginning steelheaders is to buy the finest quality monofilament. I've used and can recommend Shakespeare 7000, DuPont Stren, Berkley's Trilene XL. Other brand names are probably equally as good, and comparable in price. I've found that it doesn't pay to quibble over pennies per day for quality monofilament.

The same types of monofilament can be used on both spinning and baitcasting reels. Monofilament beats braided line four different ways for baitcasting reels and it sinks better, which makes it a tremendously useful item for baitcasting fans.

I'd hazard a guess that the bulk of steelhead spinning and baitcasting reels are spooled with twelve- or fifteen-pound monofilament. Light line men go with the four- and six-pound mono and trollers often spool ten-pound line on their trolling reels. Twenty-pound mono is commonly used on backing for flylines.

If you are a once or twice a week steelhead fisherman, you can save money by buying mono in bulk spools. The occasional fisherman is better off buying spools one hundred yards at a time.

Flylines

Flylines come in all shapes and sizes, rated by the American Fishing Tackle Manufacturers Association (AFTMA) from size 4 to 11.

The choice of a flyline is important to the steelhead flyfisherman because it is the weight of the flyline that is cast, not the fly or a lure as in all other types of fishing. The flyline must be heavy enough to bring out the power of the rod to make the cast.

Flylines are made in double tapers, weight forward, level, floating, sinking, floating with a wet sinking tip, shooting taper and sinking wet head. The shooting taper is the flyline used most often by West Coast steelhead fishermen while Great Lakes steelheaders, with their smaller streams, normally get by with either a fast sinking flyline like the Wet Cel, Wet Tip or Wet Cel Wet Head. Each line is designed to do a specific job on a specific stretch of river.

Lead core shooting heads are popular on the West Coast for deep rivers where sinking qualities are more important than casting qualities. I've used lead core shooting heads off and on for years and they sink like a rock. They also cast like a bullet, which can be damaging to your ego (and your ear) if the fly comes whizzing too close to your head. I carry one in my vest for that sometimes occasion when I'll need it, but I rarely use the critter.

The shooting taper is the flyline for West Coast fishing where long casts are often called for. The shooting taper is a thirty-foot piece of sinking flyline attached to mono running line. The taper is cast and it pulls the running line along behind making an effortless cast of seventy to one hundred feet a reality for many fishermen.

Flylines will vary in price from manufacturer to manufacturer but a good tapered flyline will cost upwards of twelve to fifteen dollars. Excellent flylines are being made by Scientific Anglers, Shakespeare and Cortland, to name just three.

ACCESSORIES FOR STEELHEADING

Show me an uncomfortable steelhead fisherman and I'll show you a man that isn't catching any fish. He's either shivering so hard or fretting so much about the pounding headache he got fishing on a shimmering summer stream, that he just cannot concentrate fully on the task of fishing.

Successful steelhead fishing is contingent on many factors, but one of the essential elements is sensible outfitting for the prevailing weather. If a sudden rain squall pops in from the Pacific our man is ready with foul weather gear. He's prepared.

Much of our better steelhead fishing comes during inclement periods of the year so this means either warm clothing, raingear, or both. To cope with the variables of weather, let's begin by dressing for a day of steelhead fishing with the thought of cold weather and possible rain or wet clinging snow.

Keeping Warm

A fisherman should wear a set of fish net underwear or "long johns" under his external clothing. Hanes and Browning are just two companies that produce excellent underwear for sportsmen. This underwear breathes well and allows accumulated moisture to evaporate without causing the wearer to feel clammy. A regular pair of shorts and T-shirt can be worn in addition to the underwear although it isn't necessary. For extremely cold weather and inactivity—winter steelheading from a boat, for example—a pair of down-filled underwear is in order. Down can be worn over the long johns for extra warmth.

A fisherman's feet are usually the first part of his anatomy to get chilled wading in ice-cold water. Begin with a pair of heavy cotton or silk stockings. A light pair of wool socks should be put on next; be sure to smooth out all wrinkles and make sure the socks aren't too tight. A lack of circulation is a primary reason for cold feet.

If moderately cool conditions are expected I usually lean toward a pair of light Levi's and a cotton shirt over my underwear. I take the down along in case it turns out cold but I don't wear it if I expect to be active. A light wool sweater can be substituted for the down.

This means you'll stay warmer during cold weather by using several layers of loose-fitting clothing than you will by wearing one or two layers of heavy tight-fitting clothes. The key point here is to keep the clothing loose and comfortable and dress from the inside out.

For cold weather conditions, I require the use of the down underwear and heavier clothing. Instead of denim jeans I much prefer either a pair of heavy corduroy pants, cut large enough to accommodate the down underwear without cramping me, and a heavy wool shirt similar to a Pendleton or Woolrich over a long sleeve cotton shirt. A cotton bandanna around your neck will prevent chafing by the wool collar. A cotton turtleneck sweater can be worn under the wool shirt and this also adds to your warmth.

Once we get past this initial two layers of clothing, differences of opinions enter into the cold-weather clothing argument. If the weather is extremely cold and blustery I generally opt for an eight-ounce snowmobile suit if my fishing isn't going to be too strenuous. If I plan on moving around a great deal I generally pull on a pair of heavy wool pants that will breathe and some type of windproof jacket. It's still essential to dress so the condensed moisture inside your clothing has a chance to evaporate and leave you warm and dry.

Your feet and head are two important things to keep warm. If you can keep your head warm, the rest of your body will also stay warm. A down hat or an old fashioned wool watch cap is usually more than enough to keep even the coolest head warm. If good visibility through slatting rain or snow is important, select an insulated cap with a long brim to keep the weather out of your eyes.

The watch cap won't keep the rain and snow out of your eyes, but it's all you need to keep your head and ears warm. In cold weather the cap can be rolled down over your ears.

For mild weather or fishing during a summer steelhead run I much prefer a baseball-type cap with a long brim to keep glaring sun out of my eyes. A long brim, combined with polarized sunglasses, will enable you to spot the flash of a turning steelhead through the glare of the water.

Your feet are vitally important to your overall comfort. Once your feet get cold, it doesn't take long for the rest of your body to follow suit. For mild fishing conditions, a pair of cotton or silk stockings and a pair of light wool socks are usually sufficient to keep your feet warm and dry. Colder weather demands further attention to your feet.

Probably the best thing I've found for warm, dry feet during winter steelheading is the felt liners often purchased for use inside snowmobile boots. Felts are one of the warmest creations known to man. They do have problems in that they absorb perspiration and as a consequence can become cold and clammy.

I've found that an initial purchase of three pairs of liners (buy them large enough to allow two pairs of loose socks to be worn on your feet) will do nicely for a two or three day trip. It usually takes one or two days to dry out perspiration dampened felts. Wear a pair of felts until your feet either become cold or they feel slightly damp. Change to a dry pair of felts and a different pair of wool socks and your feet will be as dry as toast. Place the damp felts next to some heat and allow them to dry out. With three pair of felts handy, you can change often and still have warm feet at all times. The felts should be purchased in just the right size to slip easily into waders. Be sure there isn't any slippage up and down or back and forth as you walk.

Some fishermen swear by wrapping their feet in either plastic garbage bags or in something like Saran wrap, and then putting their heavy wool socks on. It could work if there is a way for the condensation to escape.

Waders

Waders are the preferred apparel for the majority of steelhead fishermen. Some men I know still prefer to wear hipboots because they are lighter and less bulky. But the advantages of hipboots are far outweighed by the disadvantages when compared to waders. Many fishermen with hipboots tend to crowd their luck and often wind up getting wet.

Your waders should be the chest-high models—not the waist-high types, which are merely a bad compromise between chest waders and hipboots. I much prefer good rubber waders over plastic or canvas models. Rubber is much more resistant to wear and tear and is easier to patch. Waders can be bought with either a plain foot or an insulated bootfoot. The insulated bootfoot is preferable for cold weather steelhead fishing.

Always purchase waders large enough to accommodate the extra clothing needed for cold weather fishing. Your waders should have a strong draw string around the top and a quality pair of suspenders. Never forget that all-important safety belt to tighten around your waist when wading.

I once knew a steelhead fisherman who had exceptionally thin legs as a result of a childhood illness. He was tall, and as a result the legs of his waders were always too large for his legs. The first place his waders showed signs of wear was along the insides of the thighs where the material rubbed back and forth as he walked. He solved this problem with garters cut from an old car inner tube. They held the material tight to his leg and he was able to obtain much more use from each purchase.

Rain Gear

Rain gear is important to the overall comfort of a steelhead fisherman. Rain gear is available as ponchos or combination jackets and pants in rubber, rubberized plastic, rubberized canvas, and plastic. Plastic raingear is just one notch better than no raingear in my opinion. It is noisy, tears easily and the rain always seems to drip through. Rubber is efficient as raingear material, but it is heavy. Condensation often forms inside rubber garments, and you can wind up as wet as if you'd stood out in the rain. Rubberized plastic is lighter in weight than rubber and for many fishermen it represents the best investment. My choice is a rain jacket made of rubberized canvas; to me, it is the ultimate type of rain protection. It's fairly lightweight, breathes fairly well and is resistant to all but the most damaging tears.

I would not choose a poncho as steelheading rain gear. I find that wearing a poncho leaves me as wet and cold as a November rainstorm; the holes under the arms serve as funnels for incoming rain or snow. My preference is a quality rain jacket with hood.

One item of clothing often overlooked by fishermen in their eagerness to pack up and leave is a pair of gloves. I just never could develop a feel for fishing with gloves covering my hands, but fishermen accustomed to gloves should always carry two pair. When one pair becomes wet, switch gloves. To keep my hands warm and dry, I coat them liberally with Vaseline before fishing. Excess water runs off and the wind and cold weather doesn't bother them nearly as much.

A handwarmer is just the ticket on a cold, windy day. They will warm cold hands quicker than anything. Many steelheaders put one in each front pocket of their fishing vest or heavy coat. When their hands get cold, they stick their rod under their arms and bury their arms in the pockets for a few minutes.

Polarized sunglasses are an important item for any steelheader. They allow you to spot a swirl as a steelhead takes your fly and they can help spot fish in the water. Polarized glasses enable you to spot underwater obstructions as you wade and possibly prevent a nasty fall. But the most important aspect of good sunglasses is to help prevent eye fatigue and headaches.

Sunglasses come in a variety of colored lenses but I find the amber lens to be the best for fishing purposes. Fish seem to stand out sharply against the background of the river bottom and this color seems to prevent eyestrain, while they give excellent fishing vision.

A vest, to me, is an item of clothing that never seems to feel just right unless every one of the pockets is filled to the brim with tackle. Large pockets are normally filled with midday's sandwiches and possibly an apple or two. Smaller pockets abound with leader material, flies, wrap-around lead, extra spools and other often-needed equipment.

Some vests are long sleeved and are suitable for late spring or early winter fishing in moderately cool temperatures. Summer weight vests usually have no sleeves and are cut shorter to allow deeper wading. Some vests are combination vests and rain jackets and these serve admirably during winter fishing. Always buy a vest with the thought in mind about what type of clothing will be worn underneath it. For that reason, it's always better to buy a vest too large than too small.

Clothing to an avid steelheader means proper clothing for the prevailing weather conditions, and planning for changes in weather. The smart fisherman takes along extra clothes for a change and heavier clothing if the weather takes a turn for the worse. Dress properly, stay warm and you'll catch more fish.

Steelheading Strategy

To a migrating steelhead, a river is as clearly marked as a super highway. And the steelhead fisherman quickly learns that the ability to read the "signs" on a steelhead stream is one of the most profitable skills he can acquire.

Steelhead usually follow a predictable migration route up their home streams. These routes feature areas where the fish can pause overnight; other areas where fish will never tarry; holding spots where sporadic feeding is done; and resting locations where fish hold in quiet water.

READING STEELHEAD WATER

A migrating steelhead is a creature of habit. It instinctively looks for places in the stream which offer comfort, safety and to a lesser degree, food. Comfort means an area where it isn't fighting the full thrust of the river current. An upstream migration taxes the fish's energy, and steelhead must rest, preferably in an area where the current's force is broken by some obstruction.

Safety is a prime consideration for steelhead as they leave the protection of deep water in the Pacific Ocean or the Great Lakes and enter the danger-filled shallows of the streams. Shallow water fills the steelhead with caution, and it instinctively seeks out the safety of deeper water.

Deep water is a relative thing; in a river with an average depth of two or three feet, a pocket beneath a stump with a depth of three feet will hold fish. On the other hand, in deeper rivers a hole with twenty-foot depths will produce fish more consistently than neighboring pools ten to twelve feet deep.

A steelhead will usually seek out the deepest water in any given stretch of river for longer lay-over periods. Steelhead often pause and rest in a deep hole for a day or more, especially if they are waiting for milt and eggs to ripen; rivermouth holes are prime examples of deep-pool holds.

Spawning steelhead do not feed actively, although they certainly will nail a properly presented lure or bait, perhaps out of instinct. Summer and fall-run steelhead are much more active feeders than winter and early spring fish. I've seen fall steelhead pursue a minute streamer for thirty feet before striking.

Steelhead feeding stations can be pinpointed rather easily. Fish will use the same feeding positions year after year, unless a change in the river's character necessitates a move.

I once knew a summer steelhead feeding area that lay directly behind the tangled roots of a fallen birch that lay in five feet of water. School after school of steelhead would stop every year to take up a feeding station at the edge of the current. The water boiled around the roots and created a pocket of quiet water where the steelhead would pause, feed actively, and then move on. An accurate cast to the edge of this quiet soft swirling eddy always brought a strike. Then, one year a particularly violent spring freshet washed the birch downstream and completely ruined this pocket.

Feeding stations and holding lies on steelhead streams remain the same unless either man or nature changes them. Of the two, nature's changes are seldom radical and the migrating steelhead can normally be found resting somewhere else nearby. A stump or boulder being moved by a flood, a tree toppling into the river during a windstorm, or the current cutting a new pathway around an obstruction—all these events create new lies. Normally when the river makes a change, an old area will silt in and the fish will no longer frequent the same spot. But when the river changes one location, there is usually a corresponding change downstream and many times this is where the steelhead will be found.

Just what constitutes a good steelhead lie? The answer to this question is rather complex, since there are varied types of steelhead rivers. Some streams are normally slow-moving rivers with a moderately deep current, while other rivers are fast, bubbling, riffle-filled and boulder-studded flows. To become adept at reading a stream it is imperative to learn the differences between the two types of rivers.

Waterfalls are stopping points for migrating steelhead. Often they must wait at a falls like this one until rains raise the level of the river, so they can pass. *(Ontario Ministry of Industry and Tourism photo)*

A slow-moving steelhead stream will normally have occasional stretches of shallow gravel-filled water although the bulk of the river may be deeper and more uniform in nature. These types of rivers can be difficult to read. But remember, when a river is basically the same depth all over, the steelhead will often seek out an area totally different from the surrounding water. Undercut banks are hotspots where fish can find comfort, safety, and a good place to feed. Away from the main thrust of the current, the steelhead are protected from predators, and the current will wash food beneath the banks.

On a quiet, slow-moving stream, any obstruction—a huge boulder, submerged stump, or a toppled tree—often harbors resting steelhead. The fish normally take up temporary residence directly behind or alongside the obstruction in the quieter eddy water.

There is a special talent needed to translate the surface pattern of a slow moving stream into meaningful information. Boils on the slick surface of a stream are usually caused by water moving around an underwater deadhead, stump or boulder. The fisherman with the experience to read "fish" into such a boil is usually the man who catches steelhead.

Over ninety percent of the migrating steelhead will be found in about ten percent or less of the river's fishable water. This points up the basic fact that certain lies will hold fish consistently during a migration.

And remember, a migrating steelhead is looking for the easiest way up a fast stream; he doesn't want to fight the current any more than an angler likes to fight opening-day traffic to the river. The fish will swing wide of a heavy riffle rather than try to bull his way upstream through the swift current. He picks his way upstream from eddy water to eddy water, expending a minimum amount of energy in the process. These pockets of eddy water are often literally full of steelies during the peak of the upstream migrations.

Certain areas in every river will hold steelhead. The signposts pointing to these hotspots are hard to read and it takes years of experience to learn to spot these areas in any particular river. The easiest ones to spot are the tail end of pools, or "tailouts" as some steelheaders call them.

Steelhead love to lie in medium-depth stretches of river just upstream from a gravel bar. Deeper pools harbor resting fish, but it's the tails of these holes that hold steelhead willing to

A good example of a slot formed by the sides of this gorge in British Columbia. The water is pinched by the sloping rocks on each side, creating pools of swirling water both above and below, which often hold resting fish. *(British Columbia Government photo)*

strike. Look for steelhead in water three to eight feet deep at the tail of a hole where the water begins to shelve up before washing over the next bar. Often steelhead actually can be seen moving or feeding in these areas. Pinpoint casting and experimentation with different casting positions will prove which spot holds the most fish.

Narrow slots formed by boulders, submerged trees, or the riverbank and an obstruction in the water are favorite spots for steelhead to gather in. Quiet water is formed behind the obstructions or the bank, and the current sluices down through the slot with food for feeding steelhead. Slots can be well defined and easy to spot, even to a novice—or they can be cleverly hid by deep water and only a trained eye can spot the boils on the surface marking the obstructions. A fish lying in a slot is almost always an active fish, willing to strike a carefully presented lure or bait. Some slots have become almost world famous for their fish-holding capacity.

Favorite locations that I always check when fishing swift water are those areas directly in front of, behind or alongside any obstruction that breaks the current flow. Steelhead often prefer these areas, particularly if the water is five or six feet deep, and again these fish are often actively feeding. Casting in close to these snag-filled areas is courting disaster, but it takes this kind of determination to lure a steelhead out into the open.

The head of a pool or drift is often a hotspot for summer steelhead; winter fish seldom hold in these areas. Many times I've taken steelhead right on the lip where the water rushes into the pool. Steelhead will usually hold just below the lip and slightly to one side in slightly quieter eddy water. The head of a pool often has a higher oxygen content during summer months than other sections of a river.

Another steady producing area for summer steelhead is in shallow oxygen-rich riffles. The water is slightly cooler and well-oxygenated, and steelhead can often be spotted holding and feeding there. These riffles are characterized by a steady uniform depth of about three to five feet, the bottom strewn with medium-sized to large rocks and boulders. The rocks and boulders provide the cushion in which a steelhead can rest and remain comfortable.

Drifts with deep water flowing smoothly through them produce steelhead consistently. Many pools have this characteristic, but look for the main flow of current along the surface. Follow this current line and watch to see if it flows along the edge of a sandbar. Steelhead won't lie *on* a sandbar but they will lie on gravel along the edges of the bar—and they will pound anything that passes by.

Deep pools always show eddies of swirling water where the current twists and turns deliver food to steelhead from many directions. Many steelhead fishermen have learned the knack of reading the surface swirls to determine the direction of the eddy water beneath the surface. Always fish these eddies thoroughly; a fish might be lying anywhere in the eddy, so it pays to try casting from different positions.

Waterfalls or long stretches of extremely swift water act as bottlenecks for migrating steelhead. Pools or runs just below a rapids or waterfall are loaded with fish at various times during the run.

Clay banks and ledges mark stream areas where many steelhead congregate. These banks and ledges are easily spotted by their grayish or yellowish coloration. Steelhead often lie curled into a small pocket in an underwater ledge and it takes a cool hand at casting to work the bait or lure into the proper position for a strike.

Pocket water, simply described, is any small pocket of quiet water where a steelhead will pause to rest or feed on his upstream migration. Pocket water fishing comes into its own on smaller steelhead streams where migrating fish hold temporarily. On a small stream, a steelhead will utilize any area large enough to cover its back as cover.

I've taken limits of steelhead (and returned many to the water) by fishing alongside submerged logs in two or three feet of water. Fishing the logs takes a frightful toll on tackle, but it can be a steady producer of big fish.

Other examples of pocket holding water are undercut banks,

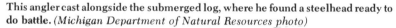

This angler cast alongside the submerged log, where he found a steelhead ready to do battle. *(Michigan Department of Natural Resources photo)*

logjams, stream improvement projects, and the like. Just remember, it takes only a foot of water to cover a steelhead's back
and a quiet place no larger than a yardstick for a fish to find
comfort and a good feeding station. Many steelies are located in
very unusual locations but these areas all afford the common
quality of adequate protection for migrating fish.

Some of the steadiest producers of steelhead are drifts or runs
over a rocky or gravel bottom four to eight feet deep. Many of
these drifts have no visible distinguishing characteristics and it
takes a great deal of practice to differentiate a productive drift
from a mediocre one.

Experimentation with new and likely-looking spots is the key
to learning more about reading a steelhead river. Never pass up
a good-looking spot without trying a few casts. A steelhead pro
once allowed as how the majority of steelhead fishermen always
fish a drift from the proper side of the river—but he said they
weren't always right. He asked me about where I stood when I
fished a certain hole. As I answered, he nodded and said that I
was fishing from the right side, but I might just catch a few
more fish by fishing it from the opposite side of the river. The
next time out I took his advice, fished from the opposite side of
the river, and caught a nice pair of steelhead: it pays to experiment.

Another pro once advised me, "Watch other fishermen like a
cat." He said they would show you their favorite spots without
being aware of it. I began watching other fishermen, especially
those catching fish, and soon found myself fishing spots I'd
never dreamed of trying before.

Once, years ago I had a hunch as I passed by a familiar,
likely-looking spot that had never produced for me. I studied
the pool for several minutes and began casting a streamer. On
my second cast I felt a soft pull of a fish that missed the Babine
Special. I made another cast and hooked a tail-walking
steelhead. What caused me to stop and fish a spot that had
never produced?

I call it "the steelheader's sixth sense"; others would call it a
hunch. I've played hunches before while steelheading and
they've often paid off big. I can't explain it and neither can anyone else but whenever I begin to feel "fishy", something happens soon after. I feel the sixth sense is something a steelhead
fisherman should work with. These hunches often revolve
around selecting a certain fly or spinner, trying a new or old and

unproductive spot, or in taking up a different casting position just a few steps away. This sixth sense has greatly increased my catch of steelhead over the years.

The beginning steelhead fisherman should always remember where he caught a steelhead, what the drift looked like, and how he fished it. As time goes on, and he catches more and more steelhead, a pattern will develop that will guide him in searching out holding water on any river. Once you've learned how to read a river, it becomes fairly easy to predict within a few feet where a steelhead will be holding. All that's left to do then is to be able to work your offering down to the fish.

PLAYING STEELHEAD

The hole was a long slanting drift with a cedar sweeper laying nearly across the river. The man had fought the steelhead for the better part of an hour, and the fish seemed uncontrollable.

The fish tried twice to bore downstream around the dangerous sweeper and into a swift, shallow run; had the steelie succeeded, it would have been a simple matter to follow the fish for 100 yards and beach him on the gravel bar below.   Instead, our angler held him strongly in a misguided notion that the fish was trying to take him into the sweeper. The fifteen-pound buck somersaulted twice at the forceful restraint and bored deeper into the depths of the hole.

When this tactic didn't work the steelhead peeled out line in an upstream run, then sulked on the bottom. The angler kept a tight line but didn't pressure the fish and it laid and rested while he stood there with an arched rod. Suddenly the fish turned and came back down into the hole, pinwheeled rapidly across the surface and finally rolled up on his side. The angler had allowed the fish to get too close to the sweeper and his line wasn't strong enough to prevent the fish from floating downstream into the entwining branches. The steelhead felt the branches poke him in the side and he wallowed and flopped on the surface until the line broke. The angler walked off muttering about how the fish took him into the tree and broke him off. Little did this misguided fisherman realize but if he'd known when to pressure the fish and when to give him his head he could have landed the fish a half-hour earlier.

When it comes to landing steelhead there are several things to remember. Learn how a steelhead reacts to the sting of a hook, how he fights, how he responds to pressure or lack of pressure and you can subdue a big steelhead very quickly. I'm *not* advocating the use of very stout line or "horsing" a green fish to the net. I've seen fishermen working in teams to horse fish. Two or three buddies wait across the river downstream from the actual fisherman. As soon as a fish is hooked, actual horsing begins: the fish makes a panicky dash downstream and the so-called angler hauls back on the rod and literally forces the fish to the surface in front of his friends. The result—a steelhead netted inside of fifteen seconds. Sporting? Hell no. I advocate the proper playing of a steelhead with conventional tackle in a sporting manner. That means using the current to your advantage and knowing when to apply pressure and when to give the fish his head. These are the keys to landing a steelhead.

Accustomed to a life in the sea or Great Lakes the steelhead is naturally wary in a stream, no matter how deep or darkly colored. He's used to being able to see for great distances through clear water. In shallow water, he's vulnerable and he knows it. To a steelhead safety lies in quick flight or refuge in a dark, deep hole, under a logjam, beneath an undercut riverbank, behind a great boulder or the like.

When a steelhead is hooked, his reaction is strong flight, inspired by absolute panic. As likely as not this initial run will be capped with a head-shaking jump. The fish may jump at any time during the run, from beginning to end. The exception, a fish hooked during midwinter's cold water conditions, will seldom jump and usually just wallow on the surface.

Many anglers make a mistake when this first run begins: they drop their rod tip and tighten up the drag. This usually hastens the fish's departure, and often results in a broken rod or line. The steelie's first run can be a sizzler, so have your drag adjusted perfectly so it starts without sticking and runs smoothly. It is important to allow the steelhead to run against the drag. The drag should be set, however, so that the fish has to work a bit to take line. The line should melt off the spool under a certain amount of tension.

If the run is a long one, always get out of the river and follow the fish downstream as fast as possible. Never *over* run your line, allowing slack line to form between you and the fish. If the fish is stationary, reel as you walk down the shoreline. Never reel while a fish is taking line against the drag; otherwise you'll wind in a monumental line twist that may cost you a lost fish.

I've found it much to my advantage to stay as close to a hooked fish as possible. This doesn't mean within five or 10 feet, but I seldom allow a steelhead to get over fifteen yards away from me. This is doubly important when fishing brushy streams. Fifteen yards of line can tangle so quickly that the line will almost always break before you have a chance to free it.

Steelhead seldom deliberately try to foul your line in a logjam or brushpile. Obstacles of this type are as dangerous to them when they are hooked as they are to fishermen. Our fisherman, at the beginning of this chapter, lost his fish not because it deliberately took him into a sweeper but because he didn't prevent the *current* from washing the exhausted fish into the debris.

When a steelhead is close to an obstruction, a combination of pressure and controlled slack is the proper course. If a fish is upstream from a sweeper or logjam and turns to come downstream, apply pressure and try to move him toward the open side of the river. Once the fish is on the proper side of the debris allow the fish to take some slack line and he'll generally shoot downstream past the obstacle. Once clear of the danger point, resume the fight in the traditional manner. When I say slack line I don't mean open the bail on your spinning reel and allow the fish to swim off with coils of mono trailing behind. Just loosen the drag slightly; the change in pressure will do the rest.

Giving controlled slack line will work well in other situations. One time I was standing on the bank of a western river once used for floating logs and I was running a chunk of fresh roe under a logjam. A hen pecked at the roe and I set the hook. She wallowed briefly and then charged off downstream with the line streaking through the water. I stepped off the bank and promptly wedged my foot between two logs. I was trapped in waist deep water and couldn't move. My fish was 75 yards downstream and still going strong. I opened my bail and removed all pressure from the fish and laid my rod and reel on the bank. The line was still floating downstream as I worked with both hands to free my foot. Five minutes later I got my foot untangled and glanced at my spool. The mono was down to the knot. As I looked a big steelhead cruised upstream on the surface about ten feet in front of me.

I climbed back onto the bank and began retrieving my line. There was no resistance as I reeled. After a couple of minutes of reeling I saw my line curving back upstream. I kept reeling as I walked upstream and suddenly saw the big hen roll up through the murky water as the line came tight. It was the same fish I'd just seen. I jabbed the hook home again and the fight resumed. Fifteen minutes later I beached an egg-laden sixteen-pound hen which I promptly released.

Many times a hooked steelhead (particularly a winter fish in very cold water) will swim upstream after being hooked and sulk on the bottom. Whenever possible I prefer to have a steelhead do his fighting upstream from me. He's easier to control when he has to fight both the current and rod to hold his position. Working against both factors will tire a fish very quickly, as long as you keep firm pressure and make him work for every inch of line he takes. If a fish sulks, a tap-tap on the rod butt will often stir it into action but I've tried this on occasions when nothing short of dynamite seems to make it budge. I've seen a few well-thrown rocks upstream from a fish pry him out of his hiding spot. The better course of action when a fish sulks is to keep a tight line and walk upstream. This changes the angle of pull and often startles the fish enough to make him move. Another trick—one I don't use myself—is to give the fish slack line, on the theory that when he feels the lack of pressure, he may move out by himself. I don't have the patience for that; I've seen fishermen wait hours for the fish to move. Sometimes they do and sometimes they don't.

Most steelheader's fishing tackle consists of a spinning or baitcasting rod and reel. With these types of reels I prefer to set my drag very loosely and apply extra drag at the proper moment with a bit of judicious fingertip or thumb pressure on the spool or arbor. When landing a fish a tightly set drag can be disastrous. More fish are lost at the net than anywhere else.

LANDING STEELHEAD

Landing a steelhead with a net can be a chancy business. I prefer to land my own, or have someone I trust do the job. I won't allow a stranger to net my fish.

Netting

To net an exhausted steelhead, place the man with the net downstream. The hoop of the net should be held motionless just beneath the surface of the water. It is up to the man with the fish on to steer the exhausted steelhead directly into the net; of course this means the fish has to be played out sufficiently to control. This crucial stage of netting calls for proper teamwork. The fish is guided downstream on a tight line to the net. When its head is over the net hoop, the angler drops his rod tip a foot or so and the fish will dive headfirst into the net. All the netter has to do is lift the net out of the water and you have your prize.

If you do find yourself netting from upstream—perhaps from a boat—hold the bottom of the net bag with the forefinger of your right hand. This hand also holds the net handle. By holding the net bag in this manner it won't drift downstream with the current and possibly tangle in the hooks of the lure as the fisherman leads the fish to net. Drop the net bag at the same time as you lift up on the net handle, and the bag will settle with the weight of the fish and you avoid any chance of a lost fish due to careless net handling.

There are as many different types of nets available to steelheaders as there are lures. I prefer to net with a twelve to fourteen-inch handle and a hoop with a circumference of approximately sixty-five inches. You can fit a tremendously large steelhead into a net of this type. The mesh should be of linear striated polyethylene, which is not subject to rotting or mildew. Avoid cotton mesh nets like smallpox. Nets with four to six-foot handles have no place on a steelhead stream, except on a drift boat.

Gilling

Gilling a steelhead is showy, but never attempt it unless you intend to keep the fish. Gilled fish seldom live. A steelhead has to be thoroughly tired out before any attempt to gill him is made. When the fish rolls up on its side within easy reach, wait until the gills flare and quickly insert two or three fingers into the gill cover and lift the fish quickly out of the water.

Beaching

Any fish that can be gilled can usually be beached. It's a safer method of landing steelhead and a beached fish can be quickly released after a brief moment of admiration.

Beaching calls for a keen sense of timing. Bring the fish toward shore on a tight line and allow the fish to bulge up a little

Gilling takes some practice, and the steelhead has to be thoroughly beaten before this method of landing can be used. *(Photo by the author)*

wave in front of it as it is led to the gravel. When this small wave of water begins to make its final crest and break on shore, ride the steelhead into shore on this tiny wave. The spasmodic kicks of the fish's tail will only push it further up the beach. Some fishermen beach their fish with a tremendous kick in the side. This is obviously injurious to the fish, especially if it is to be released, and often knocks the fish off the hook, after which it swims away to die. To me, kicking a steelhead is akin to gaffing one; a treatment I could never give such a great fighter.

Lifting

Small steelhead in the one to two-pound size can be "belly-lifted," a method devised some years ago on largemouth bass. The angler leads the tired fish over his submerged widespread hand, resting the palm of the hand across the steelhead's belly. The middle finger should point along the middle of the belly toward the head; this pushes against the internal organs and momentarily paralyzes them. They can then be lifted from the water and unhooked. Try this with a big steelhead and he's liable to slap you up alongside the head with his tail.

I release a large number of my steelhead, especially the hens, and I often do it without taking the fish from the water. A pair of hemostats furnished by a friendly doctor is great for unhooking a steelhead (a pair of needle nosed pliers will also do). Lead the exhausted steelhead within reach and reach down and take out the fly or lure with one quick twist. The steelhead will sink down, turn and swim off without having been handled.

Bait Fishing
For Steelhead

Despite the many steelhead lure innovations of recent years, drift fishing with bait is still the number one steelheading method. Steelhead feed actively on free-drifting eggs and other natural bait and fishermen have learned that a well-presented natural bait is possibly the most productive and shortest means to hanging a fish on the end of their line.

Steelhead bait takes in a wide realm of natural and artificial offerings. Single salmon eggs, clusters of unripened steelhead or salmon roe still in the skein, spawn bags, nightcrawlers, earth worms, red worms, wigglers (mayfly larvae), minnows, corn, shrimp and others fall in this category. Also included are the new artificial cluster eggs such as Luhr Jensen & Sons' J-Bait.

Bait fishing is a brand of sport designed for the patient angler; the fisherman with a sensitive touch of a safecracker and the honed skill of a person who's spent countless hours on a steelhead stream. The successful bait fisherman knows the river, the river bed, habits of steelhead, how and where to cast to present his bait properly, and has the patience of Job to wait out a finicky feeding fish.

A bait fisherman quickly learns how to detect the soft delicate take of a feeding steelie; many fishermen have developed a sort of sixth sense about setting the hook, the result of long hours of drifting bait through countless runs. I've hooked and landed many steelhead that I directly attribute to this acquired sense.

Baitfishing places heavy physical demands on the fisherman, too: he must place his casts into the proper area time after time; he needs to be strong enough to wade heavy water; and he has to couple instantly the thoughts of how his bait and weight is reacting on the river bed to his rod hand.

BAITFISHING TECHNIQUES

Most drift fishing with bait is done by the wading fisherman. With the exception of a few hard-to-reach spots, the wader can more adequately cover a drift than can a boat or shore fisherman. By expert wading, he can work his bait into places untouched by all but a few diligent boatmen.

Proper placement of the fisherman in relationship to the lie being fished is almost equally as important as placement of bait on the cast. Many beginning steelheaders walk down to the edge of a drift and throw out their bait without giving a thought to where to stand, where to cast, and where the steelhead should be lying. Expert steelheaders sometimes do this—often without prior thought—because proper placement has become an instinct and they seldom give it any conscious thought. But there are few steady fishermen, when questioned, who wouldn't agree that these three factors—where to stand, where to cast, where steelhead lie—are as important to consistent productivity as any other factor.

Many steelheaders rely solely on the across and upstream cast; this type of cast produces plenty of fish on almost every river. But it isn't the only method of fishing in the bait man's bag of tricks.

For proper body placement for the across and upstream cast, stand approximately directly across the river from where you feel a steelhead is lying. As soon as the bait hits the water, allow several coils of line to spool off the spinning or baitcasting reel. The bait must be allowed to sink rapidly to the bottom. Once the bait and sinkers touch bottom, keep a tight line and allow the bait to begin bouncing downstream. In fairly swift streams the bait and weight will just reach bottom about the time the line is directly across stream. Keep the rod tip at about a 10 or 11 o'clock position, and reel just enough to keep the line tight as it drifts downstream. A too-low rod tip will not allow you to feel the delicate tap-tap-tap of the sinkers as they bounce downstream. A rod tip held too high (12 o'clock) will be fine for feeling the sinkers bouncing and the soft take of a steelhead, but the fisherman will find it difficult, if not impossible, to set the hook firmly.

Many sections of a stream bed will have the deeper pockets steelhead prefer. If you feel a dead spot as the bait drifts downstream, drop several coils of loose line at just the proper moment. This will enable the bait to work into the deeper pocket.

The first across and upstream cast should be the longest. Subsequent casts should be shorter, closer to the opposite bank and at different angles—both upstream and across. Experiment with casting different angles until you feel you've thoroughly covered the water from one casting position.

If the drift is a fairly long one it may take several different casting angles to properly fish all the possible holding water. Each new casting position should be about fifteen or twenty yards downstream from the previous position. Work each new drift thoroughly and again experiment with different angles and locations.

As the bait and sinker bounce downstream lift the rod tip occasionally, to keep the bait skimming just over the tops of the rocks on bottom. Whenever the rhythmic tapping or nodding stops, that is the signal to set the hook. Many times it means the sinkers have lodged briefly under a rock or the line and bait is hung up on an obstruction; sometimes it also means a steelhead is taking your bait. It is better to set the hook every time with a sharp, six-inch lifting motion than to miss that one good strike of the day.

After an extended period of bait fishing in this manner the steelheader soon learns the nature of the stream bed and the whereabouts of hook-fouling debris. Close attention to where fish are hooked, where debris lies in the river and how current affects the drift of a bait will show the fisherman the best way to fish each stretch of river.

The across and upstream method of baitfishing is probably the best approach to keep from spooking a wary steelhead. The bait is presented in a natural manner while the fisherman is well away from the flow of current where he might possibly scare a fish by careless wading or rod movement.

Fishing Downstream

One of the best methods of bait fishing, and the most difficult to master, is the downstream fishing technique. Casting distances are extremely short and good wading ability is a must, in order to work into the proper fishing position.

In this downstream fishing method the angler must know almost exactly where the steelhead is laying and he must be able to wade stealthily into fishing position directly upstream from the fish. This takes some doing on a slick, boulder-studded stream, like those found along the West Coast and up into British Columbia. In some respects, wading is more important than the actual casting technique.

Once the fisherman has waded quietly into position and allowed the noise of his wading to quiet down for several minutes, it becomes time to cast. Make a short ten or fifteen-foot cast either directly downstream or slightly across and downstream. After the cast is made, the bail or freespool is left open and free line is held in the free hand. Allow the bait and weight to sink to bottom where it will hold motionless in the current. The secret of this method hinges on moving the bait directly downstream toward the steelhead. Use just enough weight to anchor the bait to the bottom on a tight line. I frequently begin with too little weight, and if I find the bait raising off bottom, I reel in and add a larger sinker. Keep experimenting until you find the proper weight for each situation. There is no shortcut or rule of thumb for selecting weight for each drift; you must use the proper weight for each spot and this calls for experimentation.

After the bait washes around downstream from the sinker for five or ten seconds, lift high on the rod tip and pull the weight off bottom. Allow the weight to drop downstream again and release two or three feet of line. The sinker will sink to bottom two or three feet downstream from its original location. Keep the line tight as you drop the bait back; many times a steelhead will grab the bait as it settles into a new location.

This method of fishing bait will enable a fisherman to drift his bait directly downstream toward any steelhead holding within six or eight feet to either side. The bait can be made to work from the left side to the right side by merely swinging the rod from one side to the other as you lift on the rod tip to drop the bait downstream.

It is possible to fish a drift directly downstream for forty or fifty yards by lifting the rod tip and walking the bait downstream with the current. But as the length of line gets longer, it becomes more difficult to detect a take. I prefer this method for short drifts of ten or fifteen yards, particularly on narrow streams where the drift may only be twenty to thirty yards long.

Casting Upstream

The upstream cast is possibly the deadliest method of bait-fishing but it certainly is also the most expensive in terms of tackle. This method also places great emphasis on body place-ment in the stream. The fisherman should be standing almost directly downstream from the suspected steelhead lie. I've found that a minimum of ten yards is needed to prevent spook-ing the steelhead, when moving into casting position for an up-stream cast. In shallow streams, where steelhead may be visi-ble, I recommend an even greater distance between fisherman and fish.

Once you are positioned, cast directly upstream far enough so your bait will be tapping along bottom as it eases into the hold-ing area. The rod tip should be at about a 9 or 10 o'clock posi-tion; reel just fast enough to keep the bait bouncing along bot-tom. Maintain a tight line at all times; reel at the same speed as the current flow.

If the bait pauses momentarily lift gently on the rod tip until you feel resistance—then set the hook. Slack line is the deadly enemy of the upstream cast, and you must pay particular atten-tion to keeping slack line from forming.

Strikes are usually difficult to detect, one reason why many steelheaders refrain from using the upstream cast. My best ad-vice is to set the hook whenever the rhythmic bouncing of the lead stops. A brief pause of only a second in the constant tap-ping should be enough indication.

Plunking

"Plunking" appeals to the more sedentary type of fisherman, and many noble West Coast and Great Lakes fishermen do nothing else.

Plunkers search out large holes or smooth runs close to the bank for their type of fishing. They cast out roe clusters and allow their bait to set motionless on bottom.

Because of the nature of their type of fishing, plunkers use large sinkers—up to 3 ounces—to hold the bait motionless in the current.

Once the bait is in the water, the rod is placed in a rod holder or the crotch of a forked stick, and all excess line is reeled up. The key to determining a strike lies in a taut line and watching the rod tip. Some anglers fasten a tiny bell to their rod tip with a small alligator clip. When a strike comes, the extra movement of the rod tip will set the bell to jingling.

Some plunkers at work—steelheading on the Kispiox River in British Columbia. *(British Columbia Government photo)*

An offshoot of plunking is the cast-and-retrieve style of plunking. Whereas the original plunking technique calls for a stationary bait, the cast-and-retrieve method calls for tossing out the heavily-weighted roe cluster and allowing it to sink to bottom. The bait is then gently inched across bottom toward the bank. The bait is retrieved very slowly and often stopped. Strikes usually occur either as the bait starts inching off, or just as the bait stops in a new location.

Some plunkers have combined their plunking activities with those of the drift fisherman by switching from heavy anchoring weights to lighter, more conventional weights. These drift-plunkers still lack the freedom of movement of the drift fisherman, but they do more casting and present a moving bait to steelhead.

Bobber Baitfishing

I've witnessed a new baitfishing technique recently, which, for lack of a better name I call "bobber-bait fishing". The fisherman has to have an intimate knowledge of the river bottom and know precisely the exact depth of the river in the area being fished. This method of fishing is rarely practiced in water over six feet deep.

The angler places a very light quill bobber far enough up his line from the baited hook so the bait will skim downstream just off bottom. Small split shot are used to take the bait down. Very little weight can be used, since the bobber will be pulled underwater.

The angler positions himself across stream from the suspected lie and casts quartering across and upstream. It is necessary to cast far enough upstream to insure the bait will be down near bottom when it sweeps through the holding spot.

The angler must keep a close eye on the bobber as it floats downstream; whenever it pauses or dips beneath the surface he sets the hook. Most steelhead taken by this method are lip hooked. Inexperienced fishermen often place too much pressure on a fighting fish, causing the line to break where the bobber is attached to the line. Another drawback is that all fish must be beached if the angler is fishing alone. If a partner is nearby, then netting is preferable.

Baitfishing at Rivermouths

Fishing rivermouths is an entirely different sport. Part of the skill of rivermouth fishing lies in being able to read the water. Each rivermouth usually has one good spot where steelhead will stack up before ascending the river. Many times they will move in to feed on free-drifting salmon or steelhead eggs that float downstream with the river current.

There usually is a spot where the river current meets the incoming wave action of the lake or ocean, creating a rip. This mixture of river and lake or ocean water is often turbulent, and the steelhead will seldom lie in such water. Instead, look near the rip for a quiet eddy where the swirling currents twist and wash the water and drifting eggs around before they settle to the bottom. This is the place to fish. Many times there will be a pocket of eddy water on both sides of the rip. It will pay to fish both pockets thoroughly.

Many rivermouths have a steep dropoff with an accompanying very distinct hole or pool, where the river current spills into open water. The edge of these dropoffs can be exceptionally productive steelhead water. Steelhead often lie along these dropoffs and pick off drifting food as it floats downstream with the river current.

Steelhead will often follow a shoreline to a rivermouth to feed. Cruising steelhead can be caught quite consistently for a mile or so up or down the shoreline from a rivermouth. It is important to find the travel route they follow.

This route will almost always be in five to ten feet of water and usually parallels a minor dropoff. Fish a piece of shoreline structure with this feature with single eggs and you can often catch your limit.

Fishing the Lakes

There are two basic methods of lake fishing: still fishing, and the moving bait technique. The majority of rivermouth fishermen subscribe to the still fishing theory, casting out single eggs and allowing them to lie motionless on the bottom. A cruising steelhead will come along and pick the eggs up and be hooked. All the fisherman has to do is keep a tight line and set the hook when he feels the gentle "tap-tap" of a feeding fish.

This particular method can be used near a rivermouth or

anywhere along the shoreline. Many fishermen wade out, cast as far as they can, keep the bail open on their spinning reels and walk back to the beach. Once on the sand they reel up the slack line and stick the rod into the sand or a sandspike and wait for the fish to strike. A trick many use is to take the anti-reverse off their reels; when a fish takes the bait, the reel handle slowly spins backward giving slack line to the fish. When the fish stops and gives a solid tap on the bait, the fisherman sets the hook.

Another way to give slack line to a cruising fish is to wrap a small rubber band around the rod handle. Once the bait is in the proper position, reel the line taut, open the bail and lightly hook a loop of monofilament under the rubber band. A steelhead will take the bait and pull the loop out of the rubber band and swim off to feed on the single eggs. This gives you time to take up the slack and set the hook while he moves off with the hook in his mouth.

I much prefer to fish a rivermouth in a slightly different manner. Still fishing seems too slow to me. I enjoy making short casts to eddy water hotspots with ultra-light spinning tackle.

Once my single egg bait and tiny split hit bottom I make one turn on my reel handle v-e-r-y s-l-o-w-l-y. I'll raise my rod tip slowly to take in slack line and reel again slowly. The object is to inch the egg bait across the bottom. Reel in six inches and let it lay motionless on the bottom. Reel again and pause. Steelhead grab this slow moving bait with a savage yank—your drag had better be set properly! This type of retrieve is hard on soft eggs but it takes only a second to rebait the hook and fresh eggs have a greater fish-catching ability.

Bait Fishing From a Boat

Bait fishing from a drifting or anchored boat can be exciting fishing. The success of drift fishing from a boat hinges on knowing where to anchor so the bait can be presented properly, and on being able to work into areas where wading fishermen never try.

Some boat fishermen prefer to walk a bait downstream directly behind an anchored boat. The downstream cast and walking technique works equally as well for boaters as for wading anglers. And many times it works better because the boat fisherman can work places in deep, heavy water impossible for the wader to cover thoroughly. The method of boat fishing I

Boaters can often fish river pools that may be inaccessible to waders; these anglers anchored above a deep drift, and worked their lures through the current—and it paid off. *(Photo by the author)*

prefer is to anchor across from a suspected hold and cast quartering across and upstream. I work the holding water thoroughly before drifting downstream about 15 yards and trying again.

Boat fishermen should fish a good drift with both methods: the downstream drift from an anchored boat, and the across and upstream cast from the boat anchored off to one side of the hold. One method or the other will almost always produce, when properly fished.

The small boat owner in a twelve to fifteen foot skiff can fish rivermouths very effectively from a position offshore. He can adopt the same methods of casting and fishing and cover more water in the process.

Chumming

Chumming is a very effective method of bringing steelhead in to your single egg bait. Throw processed salmon eggs into the vicinity of where you'll be fishing, and then fish your eggs through the same hole. The important thing is not to chum with too many eggs; you want to stimulate their appetite, not feed them. Six or eight eggs is plenty of chum.

If you are fishing just below where the river current enters open water you'll have to throw your eggs upstream in the river so they drift down into the best holding spot. Many times a small handful of chummed eggs can spell the difference between catching steelhead and just enjoying a day on the water.

STEELHEAD BAITS

Of the countless hundreds of baits and lures that can produce a steelhead strike, the eggs of a hen steelhead (roe or spawn) are probably the finest bait available to the fisherman.

SPAWN

There seem to be two schools of thought on preparing spawn for use in spawn bags (sometimes called "strawberries" or "roe sacks"). Some steelhead fishermen believe in processing the roe to keep it from spoiling, while others believe processed spawn emits a distinctive odor that deters steelhead from biting.

There are also two factions on fishing spawn; one faction likes to fish his spawn in spawn bags while the other prefers to fish with raw roe. Raw roe advocates claim a nibbling steelhead will feel the porous mesh material of the spawn bag. They say the netting can catch in the small teeth in the steelhead's mouth and cause him to drop the bag before the fisherman has a chance to set the hook. For myself, I've never known either raw spawn or spawn bags to outfish the other in the hands of a good bait fisherman.

Processing Spawn

One method of preparing steelhead spawn (which works for either spawn bags or raw spawn) is the borax powder treatment. This fine powder, available at most grocery or drug stores, is not to be confused with Boraxo. Borax powder will toughen the eggs, inhibit the growth of bacteria which will ruin the eggs and also preserve the color.

Tie the eggs up into spawn bags about the size of your thumbnail (if the eggs are loose from the skein) and place a half-inch layer of borax powder in the bottom of a coffee can or some suitable container. Place the spawn bags into the bottom of the can, on top of the borax powder, and then liberally sprinkle borax on top of the egg sacks and around all sides.

A second layer of spawn bags can be placed on top of the first layer and covered with borax powder. Repeat the process until you are tired of tying spawn bags or the can is full. Top off the top layer with a half-inch of borax powder and place in the refrigerator. If the eggs are fairly dry when you tie up spawn bags, and the refrigerator is set at 33 to 40° F, the spawn bags will keep up to a year.

Another method of using borax powder that produces a soft clustered egg bait is to lay a skein of steelhead roe onto paper toweling and snip bait-sized chunks from the skein. As the pieces are cut drop them into the borax powder and cover the chunks thoroughly. Once all pieces of roe are dusted with borax powder, place them on layers of paper toweling and cover with additional borax powder. The toweling and borax will soak up any excess moisture. A couple of days in the refrigerator will create a soft to medium-soft egg cluster which will milk well in the water. If a drier, tougher cluster is desired, increase the time in the refrigerator to several days and change the wet borax powder and replace it with dry borax and new toweling.

A baby food jar, small coffee can, or any wide-mouth jar is perfect for storing cluster egg baits. It is important to have an air-tight seal when storing cluster eggs. Clusters that will be kept for some period of time should have extra borax powder added to inhibit bacterial growth.

Curing Spawn

Many years ago I discovered an intriguing method of curing commercially bottled steelhead spawn. This commercially processed roe usually came two or three skeins to a bottle and is normally quite wet and juicy from the accumulation of egg juices and fish oil in the bottling process. Many times it was simply too soft and oily to fish with.

I found that I could air-dry it in three to six hours, depending on outside temperature and sunlight, and have enough pieces of raw spawn to fish with for several days.

My procedure was to lay several sheets of newspaper on the ground, in the sunlight, and place the skeins of eggs onto the paper to dry. It pays to check frequently for firmness. This is accomplished by pushing down on the "dried" surface with a fingertip. If the skein feels about the same consistency as your fingertip, that side is dried sufficiently and the skeins can be turned over.

Once both sides are dry, cut the skeins lengthwise in strips about three-quarters of an inch wide. Place these strips on fresh dry newspaper and allow the raw sides to dry in the sun. Turn the strips frequently to insure that all sides dry equally. Don't let them get too dry or the eggs will become crumbly and won't stay on a hook.

Once all sides of the strips are dried, cut each strip into numerous thumb-nail sized chunks for bait. These smaller bait-sized pieces must be air dried briefly to put the final firming touches to the bait. After this final step the pieces can be placed in a bait jar with an air-tight lid and will keep for months in a cool place.

The drying process can be hastened by using your wife's oven (if she'll let you) set at very low heat. A hair dryer will also work for a hurry-up job. The only way to err in using this technique is to allow the skeins to become brittle.

To prepare loose "ripe" steelhead eggs for use in spawn bags, treat the washed eggs with boric acid crystals. Boric acid crystals can be obtained from the local drugstore and they provide an effective means to prevent bacterial deterioration of the eggs.

The loose eggs should be thoroughly rinsed off with cool water to remove all broken eggs, traces of blood and other possible contaminants. Once the eggs are cleaned place them in a large bowl or pan and begin mixing in the boric acid crystals. Stir the crystals gently into the mass of loose eggs. As the eggs absorb the crystals pour more crystals in and keep stirring.

Add boric acid crystals until the eggs will not absorb any more of the chemical. The addition of the crystals and constant stirring creates quite a sticky mess. Once treated in this manner, the eggs are tougher and very resistant to spoilage. Tied into spawn bags, eggs treated in this manner will keep for months in a cool refrigerator.

Another method of preparing ripe eggs, one that involves no chemicals at all, is the cold water hardening method. Instead of washing the eggs in cool water, wash the loose eggs in ice cold

Curing spawn: dry the commercially-processed spawn in the open air for about three to six hours, until it is firm.

Then cut it into smaller strips about three-quarters of an inch wide, and allow the sides to dry out.

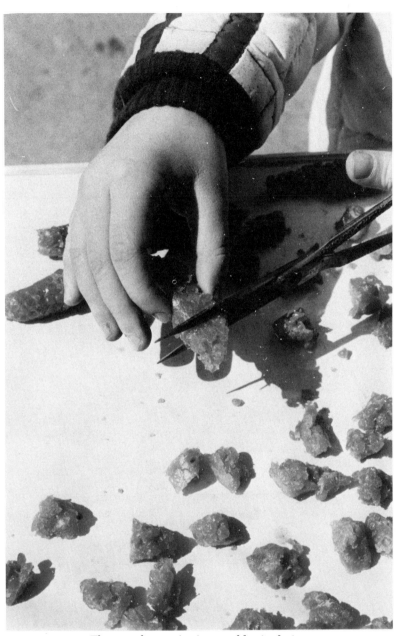

Then cut these strips into marble-sized pieces.

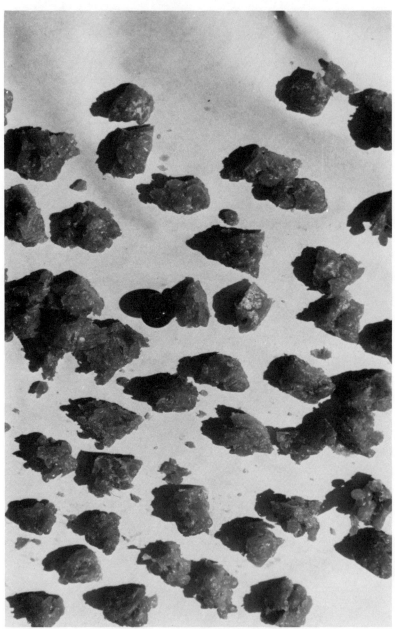

The finished cured spawn, ready for storage or fishing. *(All photos by the author)*

water. Extremely cold water will firm up the outer shell of the egg and also rinse away all traces of blood. I've found that a large bowl, filled with ice cubes and cold water, is the best way to clean and harden the eggs. Wash the eggs thoroughly and then strain through a colander.

Eggs treated in this manner must be kept extremely cold; otherwise they are subject to spoiling. Once treated they may be tied up in bags and placed either in a cold refrigerator or the freezer until it's time to fish.

Tying Spawn Bags

Many fishermen figure the larger the spawn bag, the larger the steelhead they'll catch. Under most conditions, this is not true. A spawn bag should not be any larger around than your thumbnail.

Spawn bags are tied from material such as bridal veil, nylon stocking or spawn bag material. A square of material is cut, from six to 12 eggs (depending on size) are placed on the material, the four corners are brought up, and red or orange thread is tied tightly around the bag just above the eggs. The spawn bag is made as round and tight as possible and the excess material is cut off above the thread which holds the bag together. A hook is put through the spawn bag near the thread and knot.

Learn to tie a hard tight marble-sized spawn bag, with a small knot, and you'll find more steelhead will be coming to your bait. Keep the baits reasonably small and try to keep from puncturing too many eggs when you put the bag on the hook.

Steelhead fishermen realize the important thing about fishing with spawn is that it milks a heavy scent into the water. This milking action releases the natural fish egg oils into the water and this attracts the steelhead. If it smells, looks and tastes natural to a steelhead, and is presented properly along the bottom, he'll pick up the bait.

Vaseline Balls

A new lure has recently appeared in the Midwest that is based on this principle of smell, sight and taste. In this method, fish eggs do not figure in the preparation of the bait. "Vaseline balls" are similar in size to spawn bags and are fished in the same manner. Only the smell and taste is different; they look like a spawn bag.

There are four basic ingredients to Vaseline balls; Vaseline petroleum jelly, anise oil, sperm oil and foam sponge. Grocery stores have an endless variety of colored dish washing foam sponges. I've found red, pink, orange, yellow, salmon and occasionally green to be the best colors.

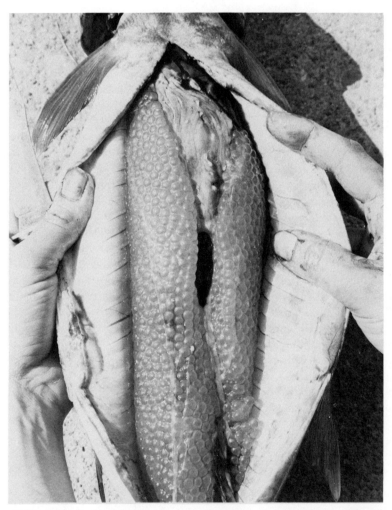

Tying spawn bags: start out with two skeins of fresh steelhead or salmon roe.

You'll also need these items handy: a pie tin to hold the slippery eggs; scissors; thread or thin wire; and nylon stocking, bridal veil material, or commercial spawn bag netting to hold the eggs.

Cut the sponge into small balls a bit smaller than a marble. The shape doesn't have to be perfect just as long as it has the basic circular shape. Normally forty or fifty balls of assorted colors will carry an average fisherman through several days on the river.

Melt enough Vaseline petroleum jelly into a metal jar lid so you have about two to three inches of melted oil. Add twelve to fifteen drops of anise oil and a similar amount of sperm oil to the melted vaseline. Stir briefly with a tooth pick to insure the ingredients are mixed well.

Drop several sponge balls into the melted mixture and allow them to soak up as much of the liquid as possible. Once the balls are saturated, lift them out and immediately drop them into ice cold water. This firms up the vaseline and seals in the odor of the anise and sperm oil.

The whole procedure will take only a half hour and most of this will be spent cutting out sponge balls. Anise oil is available in any drug store. Sperm oil is harder to find; I'd suggest check-

Spoon out six to twelve eggs onto a two- or three-square-inch piece of material.

Bring up all four corners into a tight ball the size of a marble, wrap the wire or thread around the bag several times, and finish off with several half hitches.

Four finished spawn bags in comparison to a dime. *(All photos by Richard P. Smith)*

ing with oldtime druggists or watch repair men. Sperm oil was used extensively to clean watches and clocks.

Vaseline balls are much tougher than spawn bags and they milk a distinctive odor into the water just as spawn does. When a steelhead grabs onto the sponge, it feels natural in his mouth and they usually take the bait without hesitation.

A nice thing about Vaseline balls is they smell much nicer than spawn bags. Like one fisherman said to me as I was walking along the bank of a river with two buck steelhead over my shoulder, "You smell like a Christmas cookie". But with two fish, it's hard to argue with success.

Single Eggs

Single-egg fishing for steelhead is one of the most promising methods of taking resting steelhead because all fish—steelhead included—are used to eating single eggs drifting down from fish spawning upstream. In fact, steelhead never see spawn bags, roe clusters and the like except on the end of a fisherman's line. It stands to reason that single eggs are much superior as a bait for steelhead. I've found single-egg fishing to be much more productive during fall and early winter months than during the spring, when the fish are more intent on spawning than feeding.

Eggs come in various sizes, odors, consistencies and colors to meet varying conditions. I've seen eggs of a natural color, red, orange, yellow, pink, brown and orangish-brown. All of them take fish under the proper conditions.

One of the important factors in fishing single eggs for steelhead is to select an egg with a good "milking" action in the water. Once hooked, the pierced eggs should slowly release a steady stream of natural or artificial (like the garlic) juice and odor into the water. It will take up to five minutes for an egg to completely milk out. A clear partially collapsed egg is usually milked out and should be replaced. A fresh single egg is much more effective than two milked-out eggs.

It pays to experiment with egg color. A rule of thumb among egg fishermen is to use a dark egg on dark days or in dirty water and clear or brightly colored eggs on the clear or bright days. A natural-colored egg is often best on those dead calm days when the overhead sun beats straight down from a cloudless sky. Red eggs are usually best on dark overcast days although the fluorescent colors will often produce well on a dark day.

Odor has been proven to be a definite attracting factor in steelhead fishing. Steelhead home in on strange smells in the water and one of the hottest new smells to hit the market is the garlic (!) smell offered in a clear egg by Austin-Grant. Several of the cheese flavored eggs are also hot producers.

Commercially prepared single salmon eggs come in a multitude of egg-firmness styles. A softer egg is normally used when fishing in the open water of the Pacific Ocean or a Great Lakes rivermouth. Water and weather conditions are such that a softer egg can withstand fishing use. The casting distance is normally fairly short and a lob cast will take the bait out to productive water with a minimum of effort. The bottom is normally soft or sandy and usually won't tear the egg up.

River fishing, where casts are short and pinpointed and the stream bottom is normally rock, gravel or boulders, calls for a firmer egg to meet these adverse conditions. Eggs can be tested by squeezing between your fingertips; if an egg bursts under a light squeeze, then it's probably a likely candidate for lake or ocean fishing. If the egg is firmer and tends to roll between your fingertips under firm pressure, it would undoubtedly serve the purpose for river fishing.

Making Vaseline balls: cut a soft dishwashing sponge into circular shapes about the diameter of a nickel.

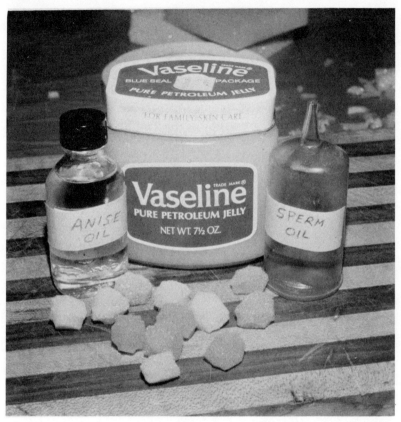

You'll also need some Vaseline petroleum jelly, anise oil and sperm oil, and an old jar top about three inches in diameter.

The Austin-Grant Company anticipated this problem and has developed a chemical formula that naturally preserves the eggs and the natural juices and still enables the customer to come up with either a firm, medium or soft egg. The Egg-Eze Kit consists of a pan, strainer and the chemical needed to process ripe coho or chinook eggs into usable single eggs for river or lake fishing.

The process itself involves washing the ripe eggs and drying them with paper towels. Broken egg skins or collapsed eggs are removed. The Egg-Eze solution is brought to a low boil and two or three cups of ripe eggs are placed into the strainer and lowered into the hot solution. The eggs are cooked at a low heat for

As the Vaseline melts, add about 12 drops of anise oil and the same amount of sperm oil.

Drop the sponge balls into the mixture and allow them to soak up as much of the liquid as possible; then remove the balls and quickly drop them into cold water.

The finished Vaseline balls not only smell good, they completely fool steelhead—and they last forever. *(All photos by the author)*

twelve to fifteen minutes and tested for firmness by piercing with a hook. The cook determines his degree of firmness by the length of time on the stove. After cooking, the eggs are rinsed in cold water, drained and dried on paper. They are then ready for fishing.

There are various methods of fishing single eggs in either open water or in a river. In the lake or ocean, where water clarity is good, the savvy steelheader will go to as light a monofilament as possible. Four pound test is about right and six pound is usually the maximum.

Since you'll be using exceptionally light line, it pays to use a long, soft rod in the 8½ to 10 foot range. A smooth spinning reel with a non-stick drag (I use a Shakespeare 2062 or 1810 reel) is needed to cope with long line-grabbing runs and sudden lunges.

Don't use too large a hook for single egg fishing. I like small hooks in number 10 to 14 size with an upturned eye, in a gold color. Eagle Claw's #479 is an excellent hook for this type of fishing. A small hook like this can be easily buried in a single egg. If you detect a fish picking up the bait and set the hook promptly, you'll generally hook it in the roof or side of the mouth. A fish that takes the bait in a slow, deliberate sucking strike will often be hooked deep in the throat or stomach.

The best way to hook a single egg is to insert the point of the hook through one side of the egg. Avoid puncturing the oil sack (the small dark spot on the egg). Move the egg in a circular motion and roll the egg onto the hook. Bury the eye of the small hook in the egg. If two single eggs are used, slide the first egg up the line before rolling the second egg onto the hook. Once the second egg is firmly hooked, slide the first egg down on top of the other egg.

A long soft rod and light line is important for making a soft "lob" presentation. This sidearm lobbing cast won't tear the bait off on the cast, and a long cast is usually neither necessary nor productive.

The single egg rig I use most frequently consists of one to four very tiny split shot crimped lightly onto the monofilament, about six to eight inches up from the bait. This method works as well in a river as it does in the lakes. Any terminal rig is only as good as the number of knots it takes to make the complete rig. A three-way swivel arrangement, or lead cinch, has three or four knots. It takes time to tie and you'll have three or four weak spots at the knots; my method has only one knot.

An arrangement many fishermen use—and one that is very productive—is the small lead egg sinker rig. This sinker has a hole through the middle; run the line through this hole and slide the egg sinker up your line and tie in a small barrel swivel below the sinker. Tie on a twelve to eighteen-inch leader to the other end of the swivel, and a small hook to complete the rig. When a fish grabs the bait and runs with it, it can take a little line through the egg sinker without feeling any drag. Many bigger steelhead will pick up the single egg, spit it out, swim back and pick it up again before swallowing. All this time they will be moving the bait away from the angler.

Baitfishing demands the utmost skill from fishermen; but those who take the time to learn how to properly prepare and fish natural baits—and where to fish them—will be amply rewarded.

Flyrodding For Steelhead

If ever there was a happy marriage intended between a gamefish and a method of fishing, it must be the flyrod and the mighty steelhead. Each complements the other, in every season of the year.

The steelhead is an outstanding adversary on a flyrod; he rips line and backing off a fly reel and makes a flyrod throb and buck as he somersaults back and forth across a river. No instrument measures the raw power of a mint-fresh steelhead better than a flyrod.

This, undoubtedly, is the primary reason more and more steelheaders are putting away their meat rods and taking up flyfishing.

Forty or fifty years ago, many anglers felt the only time steelhead could be taken on flies was during the summer run. Now sportsmen have learned that steelhead can be successfully taken at all times of year, providing water conditions are acceptable to fly fishing.

Water conditions are very important. The river must not be too dirty, swift or high to produce good flyfishing. Flyfishermen normally prefer the water temperature to be 45° F or slightly warmer; fish are more active then and will come to the fly better. Colder water makes steelhead sluggish and reluctant to strike a fly.

Choosing Fly Tackle

The proper choice of equipment is fundamentally more important to the flyfisherman than to other steelheaders. The reason is quite simple: steelhead are often found holding either against the far side of the river or behind mid-stream obstructions where a long distance cast is needed to cover them. Poorly balanced equipment simply isn't capable of making the long casts needed to catch fish consistently.

The choice of flyrod is uppermost in many anglers' minds, and here the fisherman should bear in mind the time of year and location he'll be fishing. High water periods during the winter run necessitate casting a longer line with heavier flies than for low water summer-run fish.

Fly Rods And Reels

My idea for a starter rod for winter fishing would be a minimum of 8½ feet and a maximum of 9½ feet. The rod should be balanced to throw a number 9 to 11 line or its equivalent in a lead core shooting head. The rod should carry its action approximately two-thirds of the way down into the handle. This type of rod will enable the fisherman to make long distance casts with a minimum of effort plus provide the necessary power to fight a strong fish in heavy current.

An ideal summer run steelhead rod should be in the 7½- to 8½-foot lengths but much more delicate. Summer steelhead are generally much smaller fish and do not require heavy tackle. Many steelheaders use rods balanced to throw a number 6 to 9 weight flyline and find this suits them admirably for the average summer fish.

Reels should be quality-built and something that will complement the weight of rod and flyline. A single action reel is perfectly adaptable for either summer or winter fish, although I much prefer one with a quality drag system. Any flyreel should have enough room left on the spool to install at least one hundred yards of braided Dacron backing.

Leaders

Leaders are a subject open to varying opinions but I'm a firm believer that steelhead, on the average, are not leader shy except during extremely low water summer conditions. At times like that, a sloppy cast will scare fish and a heavy leader stands out like a hawser to the spooky steelhead. Under normal late fall-winter-early spring conditions, a leader up to 12 or 15 pounds test won't bother steelhead. I used to use custom-tied tapered leaders with a heavy butt section tapered down to a 6-pound tippet for summer fish and tapered to 10 pounds for winter fish. No longer. Custom tied leaders are expensive to buy and time-consuming to tie. I have switched to six- to eight-foot lengths of monofilament in the new thin-diameter mono-filament testing 8 pounds for summer fish, and 12 pounds for winter fish. New monos are much smaller in diameter and are available in colors that are impossible to spot in the water. I generally use an eight foot leader during summer's clear water conditions and shorten the leader down to about five or six feet for winter fish.

For several years, I've been experimenting with a new twist for leader material for winter steelhead, when the rivers are high and milky or dirty from runoff or snow and ice melt. The fish are sluggish and hugging bottom. Conventional flyfishing techniques are almost hopeless.

I happened onto a spool of darkly colored braided wire line in 20 pound test. It had about the same diameter as six-pound mono. I needed some extra sinking qualities without resorting to split shot so I decided to give the wire line a try.

I tied the smallest barrel swivel made into my leader after cutting it back to about four feet in length. I then tied a Perfection Loop into one end of a three-foot length of wire. I put the loop through the other end of the swivel, pulled the standing part of the wire line through the loop and snugged the knot into the barrel swivel.

I pulled the end of the wire through the eye of my fly, tied a Turle knot and slid the knot down tight over the head of the fly. It was necessary to work the knot tight slowly to avoid kinking the wire.

Once the fly was tied I tried casting. I was pleasantly surprised to discover the thin wire didn't upset my casting and didn't overload my rod. The line shot out smooth and straight, and the wire pulled the fly to the bottom where I could feel it ticking along. Several casts later I felt a smooth strong pull, and when I tightened into the fish a buck weighing close to fifteen

The wire leader trick will allow you to get a fly down to the fish in heavy water without resorting to leadcore line or split shot. *(Photo by the author)*

pounds wallowed to the surface in the cold water. Minutes later I beached the fish, gingerly turned him around and pointed him toward deep water. The nymph had been buried in the corner of his jaw.

The wire leader trick will allow steelheaders to get down slightly deeper than before without resorting to split shot or wrap-around lead. Another aspect of wire I've learned to appreciate is that it aids in setting the hook. There is a certain amount of give in fly lines and monofilament leaders, but a two- or three-foot section of wire line anchors the hook securely on a strike. Believe me, setting the hook into a big steelhead with a wire line is like anchoring a hook into a brick wall: it jolts your arm and wrist.

Fly Lines

Since the majority of steelhead flyfishing is a long distance affair, the fisherman must be able to do two things well: he must be using a line capable of being cast up to one hundred feet, and the line must sink readily in order that he may cover the best areas in a river. A line that doesn't sink well will be pulling a fly well over the heads of most steelhead. There are times during the summer run when smaller steelhead will come to the surface for flies, but the bulk of the fishing will be done below the surface or just off bottom.

An assortment of fly lines designed solely with the long distance casting steelhead fishermen in mind are on the market. One of these is the Weight Forward (WF) line. This is a standard flyline and many steelheaders use them during the summer run when casts need to be more delicate and the fish are generally not found as far away from the angler. Weight Forward lines come in a variety of sinking types such as floaters, slow sinkers, fast sinking, wet tips and so on. Many steelhead fishermen carry extra spools with various types of sinking characteristics to cover most stream situations.

Many line manufacturers are now producing shooting heads for use on large Western streams. Very few Great Lakes streams are large enough to warrant using a shooting head. A shooting head with a monofilament running line behind the head facilitates long, relatively effortless casting. The bulk of the fishermen prefer to buy heads already made up which will balance with their rods.

It is possible to make thoroughly acceptable homemade shooting heads from a double taper (DT) flyline which will balance with your equipment. The flyline is cut roughly in half and the running line is attached to the shooting head. Just make sure you don't leave too long a length of level line at the tip or it won't cast properly. A small dab of Pliobond will make a smooth connection between mono and shooting head that won't catch in the guides as you play a steelhead from the reel. Homemade shooting heads will normally be anywhere from twenty-five to thirty-five feet in length although the average is somewhere close to thirty feet.

In recent years lead core line has been lauded as the lifesaver of many steelhead fishermen. It casts like a bullet even for long distances, sinks like a rock in the heaviest current, and is relatively inexpensive to make.

I have a personal aversion for fishing with lead core shooting heads. I take an active dislike to that much weight whistling shrilly by my ears. I've taken a couple of whacks in the back of the head with a lead core shooting head that felt as if somebody had practiced a karate chop on my noggin.

The best way to make up a lead core head is to weigh out lead core trolling line on a bullet reloader's or druggist's scales. Determine what weight line will balance your rod and reel by consulting a line manufacturer's list of specifications or an AFTMA (American Fishing Tackle Manufacturers Association) chart. Once you've got the proper length, cut the line, connect the line to the monofilament running line and you're in business.

Casting a shooting head takes a bit of practice. The proper technique is to work the head out until it is about three or four feet past the rod tip. Lift the rod tip sharply to pull the line from the water, false cast the shooting head once or twice and let fly. The shooting head will take off, pulling the monofilament running line behind, and anyone with any experience at casting can automatically add twenty to thirty feet to his previous best efforts with this technique.

Anglers adept at double hauling will be able to greatly increase their line speed and distance by applying the haul to the shooting head. In fact, the bulk of the Western steelhead fishermen rely on shooting heads and the double haul to place their flies in range of steelhead. The double haul will enable the skillful caster to make ninety to one hundred-foot casts with practice.

FLY FISHING TECHNIQUES

Fishing conditions vary greatly between summer and winter-run steelhead, as we have seen. The rivers are lower and clearer, and the fish generally smaller during the summer than during the highwater periods of winter. The flyrodder seeking steelhead action must choose his tackle and fishing techniques accordingly.

There are many techniques for presenting a fly to a winter steelhead, but whatever stream conditions prevail, the fly *must* be presented near the bottom. This is extremely important to remember, especially when the water is very cold.

West Coast fishermen follow a certain sequence. Flyfishermen pick certain known areas where fish normally hold and as many as fifteen or twenty fishermen comb the stretch. The flyfishermen will normally begin at the top of a pool and slowly work downstream. Two or three casts in one area are usually sufficient, then the angler moves downstream about ten feet and begins casting again. Once he's worked through the best water he'll often wade upstream and begin working the drift again.

The practice most fishermen follow is to begin covering water closest to them and lengthen each cast until all water within casting distance has been covered.

Most winter steelhead are taken by a casting quartering across and downstream. The sinking capabilities of the flyline or shooting head will take the fly moderately deep in swift current. A steelhead holding in a pocket behind a boulder will spot the fast-swinging fly as it passes above or in front of him. Repeated casts to the same spot will often trigger the strike response from a resting fish. Steelhead strike a fly swinging across the current savagely. Jumps often follow a flashy, hard strike.

I seldom give any action to a fly because the water current will give the fly most of the action it needs. Occasionally I'll twitch the rod tip or the line with my line hand, although I have taken only a few fish by using this technique. Other anglers tell me steelhead often strike just after they twitch the line.

A variation of this across and downstream cast would be to use either a slow sinking or a floating line with a sinking tip. The fly is cast across and downstream but the flyline is mended upstream as often as necessary. This slows the drift of the fly and presents it to the steelhead in a more broadside manner. A take on this type of cast is often more deliberate, not the yank-splash type of strike normally associated with the conventional type of across and downstream cast. The steelhead often rises off the bottom and takes the fly broadside in his mouth in much the same manner as a fish grabbing a minnow.

Another trick is to allow the fly to hold momentarily downstream before lifting it out. Many steelhead will follow the drifting fly without taking but if the angler adds a bit of rod tip action to make the fly dart and wiggle before lifting it from the water, he may draw a strike. It's a trick worth trying at the end of every cast.

A special winter steelhead technique I've often used is the direct or quartering across-and-upstream cast. This works well in medium-depth drifts that are neither too swift or too slow.

The cast is made as far as possible upstream and still enables the fisherman to maintain control of his line. As the current sweeps the fly deep into the holding water, the fisherman will recover enough line to be able to detect the delicate take. I've found the gentle twitching of the rod tip will create a lifelike movement to a fly and steelhead often take in a slow confident manner.

The upstream cast allows the fly to work much deeper than a cast quartering across and downstream. The important thing to remember is to keep the line as tight as possible as it drifts downstream. I normally watch my flyline where it enters the water. If it pauses, even momentarily, set the hook because a steelhead may have picked up the deep-drifting fly.

Nymphing

In fact, I often use nymphs during cold weather periods because I firmly believe a nymphal imitation to be far superior on many streams to a more classic streamer or wet fly.

Nymphing calls for a keen sense of observation and a sixth sense about strikes. I was fishing an Ontario stream early one year and snow banks lay heavy in the woods. The steelhead season was open but the weatherman had forgotten about spring.

I was easing down a stretch of the Agawa River and casting brightly colored streamers and wet flies into likely spots. Nothing came to my flies, although I could plainly see steelhead holding in the deeper holes. The water was extremely cold, about 35° F, and the fish were loggy and uninterested.

I finally sensed that bright colors were a waste of time and switched to a dull Spring's Wiggler. I turned my attention to casting upstream with a long line and lengthy leader tapered down to six pounds.

I poked cast after cast into deep pockets and occasionally I saw the flash of a silver side as a steelhead moved away from the intruding nymph. Finally, after exhaustive casting, I saw the flyline switch sideways and I lifted the rod tip gently and barbed a sparkling fresh fish.

The male had just the faintest hint of pink along his flanks and the stripe glistened in the sun as he uncorked an acrobatic leap across a tree limb jutting into the river. The buck snapped the leader and was gone. Two more holes produced two more strikes and one beached male fish weighing seven pounds wore the nymph like a tiny mustache on his upper lip. Another fish, a female, had been hooked and lost after a thrilling five-minute battle. All the fish were the same approximate size.

There is another nymph method that works almost as well on steelhead as on other trout; the nymph is cast across stream and fished on a dead drift. Medium-depth pools are the primary places where this method produces best.

Another variation is the upstream cast with a deep-sinking dead drift. The important thing here is to get the nymph right down to the gravel. Once the nymph reaches bottom and is approximately across stream from you begin a gentle inch-by-inch jerking retrieve as the fly works downstream. The nymph will scuttle across the bottom like a real nymph. This has been a deadly producer for me at various times.

Flyfishing the Beds

Although many of the traditional flyfishing methods work equally well on Great Lakes or Pacific streams, there is one Midwest invention which is especially productive during late winter and early spring when steelhead move onto the beds to spawn.

Wading expertise is essential in all forms of flyfishing, but fishing for bedding fish calls for a highly developed skill in getting close to the fish without scaring them.

Walk the banks and look for fish on the redds (I wear polarized sunglasses to cut the glare and to enable me to see fish beneath the surface). Once the spawning fish are spotted, you must decide on your approach.

Flyfishing the beds requires concentration and exact presentation. A stealthy approach and a well-executed cast are especially important when casting streamers downstream, as this angler is doing. Note that he's also wearing polarized glasses to help locate the spawning fish. *(Photo by the author)*

There are two methods of streamer presentation; the upstream and downstream casts. Although the upstream cast produces the bulk of the fish for many sportsmen, I feel the downstream cast to be more exciting. The secret lies in easing into casting position without spooking the fish. Most Great Lakes streams are shallow and brushy so this necessitates working slowly into casting position, often only twenty or thirty feet away from the fish.

Once you are directly above the steelhead, or above and slightly to one side, make your cast quartering across and downstream. Work the streamer directly to the fish. A splashy cast or repeated false casting will spook these wary fish. A stealthy approach and a clean, well-executed cast are the keys to success.

As soon as the fly swings past the fish's bed, lift it out and make the cast again. I've found it often pays to give the rod tip a little twitch just as the fly swings in front of the steelhead. If a fish turns and follows the fly from the bed, it's a sure bet it will strike.

The key to the success of this downstream casting approach to bedding fish is to read the speed of the current, its depth and to be able to cast to a small spot. Hit the right spot time after time and your fly will be skipping along the gravel when it approaches the steelhead. Do this enough times and you'll catch fish.

The other approach to this type of flyfishing is the upstream cast. It produces more steelhead solely because most anglers are approaching their fish from behind. A lengthier leader is called for because you must cast the fly upstream past the steelhead, allow it to sink and work it past the fish's nose. A short leader means the end of the flyline will land on top of the steelhead.

Depending on the speed and depth of the current, cast anywhere from six to 10 feet upstream from bedding fish. Keep a tight line as the fly drifts downstream. Set the hook if you see a steelhead move whenever the fly is near. I've seen steelhead suck a fly in from two feet away just like a largemouth bass inhaling a plastic worm. You'll seldom feel the strike in this type of fishing. A movement on the part of the fish is often the only clue you'll have to setting the hook.

Many times the redd will be deep enough so that the lure or fly will pass over the fish. If this is the case, drop a foot or two of slack line just as the lure comes to the redd, and it should fall right in front of the fish's nose.

A spinner is also excellent lure for provoking a strike, although a streamer or wet fly will do just as well. It's the aggravation of the lure more than its appeal as food that counts, and the fish strike out of anger or redd protection, not because they're hungry. Once in a while a spawning buck will chase a lure or fly out of the bed, but he will seldom strike at this time. Most often strikes occur just as the bait drops into the bed or passes between the spawning fish. Watch for a sidewise movement of the steelhead's head, and strike whether you feel the fish or not. Often you'll be rewarded with a slugging go-round with a big fish.

Summer Fly Fishing

Summer-run steelhead are usually much smaller fish than their winter cousins—averaging 3 to 6 pounds—but what they lack in size they make up for in hard strikes and high cartwheels.

The heavy lead-core or sinking lines or shooting heads are generally not needed. Tackle is more sophisticated and a skillful presentation is more important than long distance casting.

It's during the summer run when the occasional steelhead will come to the surface for a drifting dry fly. This occasion isn't something an angler can build a fishing trip around—it simply doesn't happen often enough. Most summer steelhead will come closer to the surface for a wet fly or streamer than they will during cold water periods. Many steelheaders simply carry an extra spool of floating line to handle those odd circumstances when steelhead are taking off the surface. A floating fly line with a sinking tip will handle many of the summer flyfishing problems.

More Flyfishing Techniques

The greased line method of steelhead fishing is something our fraternity has adopted from Atlantic salmon fishermen. The floating flyline and leader is thoroughly greased, to keep it floating high and dry. A very sparsely dressed wet fly or small streamer can be fished just beneath the surface of the water with a drag-free drift. The angler must constantly mend his line upstream to remove any line bellies formed by the current, which causes the fly to swim just under the surface in an enticing manner.

Another adaptation to steelheading from the lore of Atlantic salmon fishing is the Portland Creek Riffling Hitch. A sparsely tied fly similar to a low water Atlantic salmon fly is knotted to the leader in the traditional manner. A half hitch is then tied at the side of the fly head. This hitch will cause the fly to swim through the surface film of the river and leave a small wake. There are times—not too often, admittedly—when this trick will wake up an otherwise dormant steelhead.

The dry fly angler often gets his best shot at steelhead early or late in the day when the fish are holding either at the head or tail of a pool. Once the steelhead drop into the depths of the pool they must be fished in more traditional manners.

Even then, it pays to experiment when all conventional methods of fishing have failed to produce. One time I was fishing the Klamath River in northern California and the steelhead present were obviously disinterested in anything I threw at them. I switched patterns, sizes and went from streamer to wet fly to nymph: nothing. Finally, in exasperation, I slapped the fly down hard on the surface over a fish holding just behind a boulder. The fish swirled upwards at the fly, made a head-to-tail rise to the floundering wet fly, and then surged back toward bottom. He didn't take. I quickly tried the same cast again and this time the fish took without hesitation.

I tightened into the fish as it peeled off for bottom and the hook sank home. We pranced up and down the river for ten minutes before I slid the fish onto the gravel, worked the fly out and put him back into the river to fight another day. I've tried that trick several times and only one other time has it paid off for me. But, when fish are coming slow, any trick that produces a strike is worth trying. To me, the magic of steelhead fishing is totally encompassed in the sport of flyfishing. There is absolutely nothing that captivates my soul as much as watching a bright steelhead come to a well-executed cast, surge into the rod with a powerful strike, and as I stand almost in awe, completely destroy the peaceful calm of a beautiful stream.

I'm hooked.

STEELHEAD FLIES

The origin of steelhead flies seems to be lost in history, although many anglers feel Zane Grey and his writings about the wondrous fishing on Oregon's Rogue River had much to do with bringing flyfishing and steelhead flies to the attention of sportsmen. Grey frequented the Rogue during the early 1920's and it was here that flies crept out of early steelheading gloom and into prominence.

Steelhead flies fall into several different categories and each type serves a specific purpose to the fisherman. The different types of flies are streamers, bucktails, hackle patterns, nymphs and the Comet-style fly.

Streamers are tied to represent baitfish that steelhead have been feeding on in the ocean or the vast expanses of the Great Lakes. A streamer is an effective fly during late winter and early spring months for dark, heavy water. But a streamer needn't be large to be productive. Actually smaller streamers produce surprisingly better results than their larger brothers. Many streamers are bulky-looking patterns that offer a larger target for steelhead to home in on in murky water.

This hen steelie was taken on Oregon waters with a simple yarn fly. *(Oregon Wildlife Commission photo)*

A close-up of the yarn fly, a simple tie that works well on both Great Lakes streams and the Pacific Northwest. *(Photo by the author)*

The Stanley Streamer is an invention of Michigan's Stan Lievense, a former fisheries biologist for the Michigan Department of Natural Resources. Stan took a small streamer and added a plastic actionizer scoop to the head of the fly. When worked in medium to heavy current the fly has a built-in wiggle that fish find difficult to pass up. In slow current, action can be provided by a well-regulated hand retrieve.

Bucktail steelhead ties resemble small forage fish to a feeding or agitated steelhead. A variety of colors and sizes of bucktails should be included in every steelhead fisherman's fly box. They often fill a necessary gap when more conventional ties fail to produce.

Hackle patterns are steelhead flies without wings, and they figure significantly in my annual catch of fly-hooked steelhead. These flies are easy to tie up and an amateurish job often produces the same satisfactory result as a professional tie. I suppose a hackle fly represents a struggling nymph more than any other food source although many hackle patterns resemble nothing a steelhead ever sees.

Nymphs are steady producers of fish, particularly during late winter and early spring months when a steelhead has his nose buried in the gravel. These wingless bodied flies are generally tied to represent one of the nymphs common to the river being fished. Most nymph patterns are dull-colored, ugly to look at but delightful in their appeal to sluggish fish.

One of the newest and most productive flies for steelhead is the Comet type. Comet flies are peculiar because the greatest emphasis is placed on making the tail of the fly the largest and most important feature. Most steelhead flies either have no tail or just a few wisps to "make the fly look right". A tail is usually just a decoration on many steelhead ties and altogether absent on many others.

Dry flies are occasionally used by steelhead fishermen for those extremely rare instances when steelhead are rising (usually summer run fish) to the surface. A small box of flies would normally cover this rare but happy occasion.

Tying Steelhead Flies

Steelhead flies range in size from smallish number eight up to the larger number two for summer run fish. Winter steelheading calls for flies tied on hooks from a six up to 1/0.

There are many times when a sparsely tied low-water fly will out-produce a bulkier tie. A sparsely tied fly will get to the bottom quickly. Flies with yarn bodies are the slowest sinkers.

Steelhead flies, for the most part, must be fished right down on bottom. This necessitates either a heavy wire hook to help sink the fly, or lead wire added to the shank of the hook as a tying step. Even though steelhead fishermen seem split in the argument of weighted versus unweighted flies, I personally favor slightly weighted flies. I find they produce just as many fish on a given day as an unweighted fly. Some flies can be made to sink a bit more readily by the addition of liberal amounts of head cement to various parts of the fly, or by tying sparsely or with flashy tinsel.

Steelhead flies are conspicuous by their numbers; in this list, I've tried to avoid the marginal producers, and list just those currently in favor and producing the bulk of fly-caught steelhead.

Fly patterns vary from the West Coast to the Great Lakes area and this chapter will list the favorites from each area separately; many of these patterns are interchangeable.

West Coast Fly Patterns

Black Demon: Tail - golden pheasant; Body - gold; Hackle - orange; Wing - black bucktail and jungle cock.

Boss: Tail - Black Polar Bear; Body - Black chenille; Ribbing - flat silver tinsel; Hackle - long fluorescent orange; Wing - none; Head - white thread.

Gold Comet: Tail - fluorescent orange polar bear; Body - flat gold tinsel; Ribbing - none; Hackle - mixed fluorescent orange and yellow; Wing - none; Head - yellow thread.

Golden Demon: Tail - golden pheasant crest; Body - gold tinsel; Ribbing - none; Hackle - orange; Wing - brown hair; Head - black thread.

Fall Favorite: Tail - none; Body - flat silver tinsel; Ribbing - none; Hackle - fluorescent red; Wing - fluorescent orange polar bear; Head - white thread.

Eel Optic: Body - silver tinsel; Wing - red bucktail; Head - large head painted white. Eyes painted red and black optional.

Mickey Finn: Body - silver tinsel; Wing - red and yellow bucktail layered with jungle cock; Head - red thread.

Orange Shrimp: Tail - golden pheasant; Body - brown spun fur; Ribbing - silver tinsel; Hackle - orange; Wing - gray mallard flank; Head - orange thread.

Polar Shrimp: Tail - red hackle; Body - orange wool; Hackle - orange; Wing - white polar bear; Head - orange or pink thread.

Royal Coachman: Tail - fluorescent red hackle; Body - red fluorescent chenille; Butt - thick peacock herl; Hackle - brown; Wing - white polar bear; Head - black.

Silver Comet: Tail - fluorescent orange polar bear; Body - flat silver tinsel; Ribbing - none; Hackle - fluorescent orange; Wing - none; Head - white thread.

Skykomish Sunrise: Tail - fluorescent red and yellow hackle fibers; Body - fluorescent red chenille; Ribbing - flat silver tinsel; Hackle - fluorescent red and yellow; Wing - white polar bear; Head - white thread.

Thor: Tail - orange; Body - red chenille; Hackle - brown; Wing - white bucktail; Head - black thread.

Umpqua: Tail - Red and white polar bear; Body - rear half yellow wool and front half red chenille; Ribbing - silver tinsel; Hackle - brown; Wing - red and white polar bear; Head - black thread.

West Coast flies: (top row) Boss, Gold Comet, Black Demon, Golden Demon; (second row) Fall Favorite, Eel Optic, Mickey Finn; (third row) Polar Shrimp, Orange Shrimp, Thor; (fourth row) Silver Comet Skykomish Sunrise, Umpqua; (fifth row) Royal Coachman, Van Leuven, Wooley Worm; (sixth row) yarn flies. *(Photo by the author)*

Van Lueven: Tail - red bucktail; Body - red wool; Hackle - brown; Wing - white bucktail; Head - black thread.

Wooly Worm: Tail - gray hackle tip; Body - black chenille; Ribbing - gold tinsel; Hackle - gray palmered; Head - black thread.

Yarn flies: Tail - none; Body - fluorescent red, orange or yellow; Hackle - fluorescent red, orange or yellow; Head - red thread.

Great Lakes Patterns

Babine Special: Tail - red calf tail; Body - red chenille; Hackle - red; Wing - white calf tail; Head - red thread.

Betsy Special: Tag - silver tinsel; Tail - red calf tail; Body - rear two-thirds black chenille and front one-third red chenille; Wing - black calf tail; Throat - black calf tail; Head - black thread.

Cowichan: (low water fly) Tail - yellow floss lacquered; Body - fat red chenille; Hackle - white calf tail; Head - red thread.

The Crick: Tail - black calf tail; Body - rear one-third fluorescent pink chenille and front two-thirds black chenille; Throat - black calf tail; Wing - white polar bear with black calf tail on top; Head - red thread.

Doctor Rex: Tail - chartreuse wool tied at front and back; Body - red chenille; Hackle - red tied in the middle of body and white hackle at front of body; Head - red thread.

Hot Head: Tail - fluorescent pink synthetic yarn; Body - fluorescent pinkish-red floss; Wing - fluorescent pink synthetic yarn; Head - red thread with tuft of wing material protruding.

Little Manistee: Tag - silver tinsel; Tail - hot orange calf tail; Body - rear two-thirds pink chenille and front one-third black chenille; Wing - one-half hot orange and one-half yellow (orange on top); Throat - hot orange calf tail; Head - red thread.

Orange P.M. (Pere Marquette) Special: Tag - silver tinsel; Tail - hot orange calf tail; Body - rear two-thirds hot orange chenille and front one-third black chenille; Wing - one-half hot orange and one-half yellow (orange on top); Throat - hot orange calf tail; Head - red thread.

Platte Special: Tag - silver tinsel; Tail - red calf tail; Body - black chenille; Ribbing - silver tinsel; Wing - yellow calf tail; Throat - yellow calf tail; Head - red thread.

Red P.M. Special: Same as Orange P.M. Special only rear two-thirds of body is red.

Richey's Platte River Pink: Tail - pink calf tail; Body - pink chenille; Ribbing - silver tinsel; Wing - white polar bear; Throat - pink calf tail; Head - red thread.

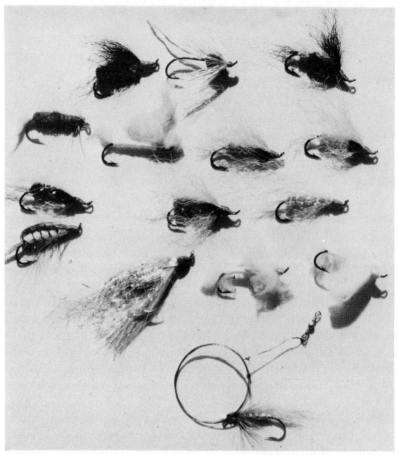

Great Lakes flies: (top row) Betsy Special, Cowichan, Crick; (second row) Dr. Rex, Hot Head, Little Manistee, Prange P.M. Special; (third row) Platte River Special, Red P.M. Special, Richey's Platte River Pink; (fourth row) Spring's Wiggler, Baby Rattler, White and Chartreuse Yarn flies; (bottom) Richey's Platte River Pink on a wire leader rig. *(Photo by the author)*

Spring's Wiggler: Tail - fox squirrel; Thorax - fox squirrel tied in at back; Body - yellow wool or chenille; Hackle - brown tied palmer; Thorax - fox squirrel tied in at throat; Head - black thread.

The angler should bear in mind that although it pays to have a fair amount of flies available for use, it is just as important to have these flies available in different sizes. I've known days when a number 4 Golden Demon wouldn't produce a touch but a switch to the same fly in number 8 would result in the strike I was looking for.

Some type of balance should exist between brightly colored flies and darker ties. Strive to have a good representative selection of each type and color pattern available.

An extremely good case can be made for using black flies. I've had very good success with all black flies under all conditions ranging from low clear water to dark runoffs. Steelhead seem very attracted to black flies during dirty water conditions.

Over several exhaustive years of steelhead flyfishing I've come to the conclusion that there is no best color for everyday use. One day a red will produce while the next day a blue- or orange-tinted fly will work best. Saturday steelhead are suckers for fire red or orange; Sunday morning, under similar circumstances, a dusky colored nymph will be the only thing that will turn Mr. Steelhead on.

Spinning For Steelhead

Spinners are considered to be one of the most productive steelhead lures available. They have a built-in fish catching action, enough heft to pitch halfway across the largest river and come in a variety of colors and sizes to match any existing water condition. A spinner can be fished deep and slow or shallow and fast. On the better spinners the blade will revolve with a pulsating throb at the slowest retrieval speed. A steelhead fisherman should learn several of these different retrieval speeds and adapt them to his daily fishing routine; many times it pays big dividends to experiment with different retrieval speeds when steelhead are reluctant to strike.

Over twenty years ago, when I was just cutting my steelhead teeth, my tackle consisted of one of the original Airex half-bail spinning reels and a six-foot rod. My lure was a European spinner of some forgotten type, which I was casting halfway across the river and retrieving rapidly back across the surface. An elderly fisherman stopped by, inquired about my luck and watched quietly for several minutes without speaking. Finally my ineptitude apparently caused him to speak.

"Young feller," he said, "you're never going to catch a steelhead by cranking that spinner across the top of the water. Get it down on bottom where the fish are." With that he grabbed my rod and reel and made a bullet-like cast across and upstream, fed a few coils of free line out to allow the spinner to sink and began a slow dignified retrieve. The spinner curled deep through the hole, swung slowly through a downstream eddy with a gently throbbing blade and then stopped sharply. The oldtimer set the hook and a gleaming silver hen steelhead rocketed into the air.

My counselor thrust the bucking rod into my hands with a sneer and asked me if I'd learned anything. I nodded my head up and down while the steelhead tore the pool apart. Ten minutes later I slid the 12-pound fish into a waiting net, and the first of many steelhead had fallen to the first of many spinners. Since that time I've experimented with sizes, shapes, colors and added weights to spinners and have come up with some definite conclusions as to what type of spinner, blade color, and retrieve turn a steelhead on.

SPINNING TECHNIQUES

The single most effective steelhead spinning method is the direct upstream cast. This variety of cast is a tackle-grabber, but it's also an efficient fish producer. The key to this method is a slow retrieve and the ability to read the water well enough to pinpoint a steelie's whereabouts. It also pays to practice this particular cast in drifts in which you know exactly where all snags are located. This cuts down on the high spinner mortality rate.

Once a steelhead lie has been determined, take up a good casting distance directly downstream. This technique works most effectively in narrow rivers or in larger rivers in which the angler can wade to the best casting position.

Cast the spinner about ten or twenty yards directly upstream from the suspected lie and allow the spinner to sink slowly with the current. Unless the current is extremely swift the spinner should be twinkling along bottom by the time it reaches the spot where Mr. Steelhead is lying. As the spinner drifts downstream with the current, reel just enough to keep a tight line and to keep the spinner blade barely turning over. A madly whirling blade will scare more steelhead than one that pulsates with a slow, throbbing beat.

Keep the rod tip low; the spinner should be felt ticking along the gravel as it bounces downstream. As the spinner passes the suspected lie, turn with the rod and follow its continuing downstream progress. As it straightens out below you, bob it gently in the current by lifting the rod tip and retrieve it swiftly. A steelhead will strike either as it passes through his holding spot, or as it swings around on a tight line below you.

If the spinner stops on its downstream drift raise the rod tip slightly and it will usually lift off the bottom and continue its downstream travel.

It should be pointed out here that casting spinners directly upstream necessitates constant touching up of hook points with a hone or file. Bouncing spinners on gravel can dull or break off the hook points, which can result in a lost fish.

River fishing requires an active imagination and a sense of originality. A bit of thought on the subject and some experimentation will often result in extra strikes and more fish. Look over a pool or run and try to decide whether there may be one or more proper ways to fish it. Some types of water will offer several avenues of approach with the spinner. If one angle doesn't work, switch positions and try another until you find a winning approach. Often a change of angle will cause a steelhead to strike a spinner that he's been ignoring.

Another method of spinner fishing that is a consistent producer is the across and upstream cast. But unless particular care is paid to the spinner, this approach will result in the spinner often not coming close enough to bottom to be effective.

Take a casting position slightly upstream from where you suspect steelhead to be laying and cast quartering across and upstream. Allow the spinner to sink on a relatively tight line and try to keep the spinner bouncing along the bottom as it drifts downstream. Keep the line tight and retrieve just enough to keep the spinner blade turning over. Fish with your rod tip at a 9 or 10 o'clock position and anytime the spinner stops, set the hook with a sharp lift of the wrist. Many times you'll feel the spinner pause slightly on some obstruction on bottom. Lift the rod tip lightly and walk the spinner over the debris. Many times a strike will come as you lift the spinner free.

As the spinner works down through the depths of the hole or run, keep a tight line to keep the blade working. Allow the spinner to swing downstream on a tight line and arc around below you. If the spinner passes through eddy water at the time, that is often one of the best spots to hit a steelhead.

Steelies seem to be great *followers* of spinners at all times of the year, except possibly during the extremely cold winter weather. I've seen steelhead pursue a twinkling spinner for twenty yards without striking. I've also seen active summer-run fish chase a spinner across a shallow drift and pound the lure several times before becoming hooked.

Many flyfishermen have taken to carrying two outfits—a spinning rod with a spinner and a flyrod. They use the spinner to locate feeding steelhead in deep water. The spinner—often barbless—is worked thoroughly through good holding water, while the fisherman watches closely for the flash of a silver turning side or the swift lunge of a striking fish. Once good fish are located, the flyfisherman forsakes his spinning outfit in favor of the long rod. He then works his streamers and wet flies through the water in hopes of landing the fish he's located.

Fishing Downstream

There are times when a conventional upstream or across and upstream method won't work. I've seen steelhead, visibly feeding behind protruding boulders or in pocket water, refuse a spinner presented in this manner. Careful wading can often work an angler to within ten or fifteen yards upstream of these feeding fish. Try to select a spinner with a blade comparable to the color of whatever the fish are feeding on.

Standing upstream from feeding steelhead, especially in a swift-flowing stream, requires the use of split shot or pencil lead to get the spinner down deep enough to be effective. The spinner must be bouncing bottom when it drifts into the pocket of quiet water where the steelhead are feeding.

The first cast is always designed to determine whether enough weight is on the line to take the spinner down to the bottom. Careful experimentation is needed to keep this weight just right to provide a tumbling action without anchoring the spinner to the bottom.

Once the weight is determined, cast to the far side of the steelhead and just slightly downstream from the fish. The current will work the spinner across and slightly upstream (that's right) directly to the fish. The spinner will approach the fish from the rear and they'll often turn and strike the intruder.

If a strike doesn't come as soon as the spinner washes into their holding pocket, reel in just enough line to position the spinner in front of their nose. Often just the turn of the reel handle is enough to move the spinner a few inches, which will increase the pulsating beat of the blade and the fish will strike viciously.

This method's success hinges on the angler's ability to wade carefully into position, to be able to read the strength and flow of the current and to cast accurately. Of course, seeing or knowing the fish are present in the first place is of great importance. A pair of polarized sunglasses are a tremendous aid in that respect.

Spinners On The Beds

Spin fishermen in the Midwest have devised a method of fishing with flyrods that produces steelhead action during the spring spawning run. Spawning steelhead are located by walking the riverbanks and searching for the glittering white redds of actively spawning fish. Once fish are located, the spinner fisherman wades into casting position directly downstream from the fish. A flyrod and flyreel with level monofilament is used because it gives the fisherman many more casts per minute than a man with a spinning outfit. A nickel-sized copper Colorado spinner—without weight if possible—is at the terminal end.

The angler takes up a casting position and begins casting the spinner about ten feet directly upstream from the spawning fish. The spinner is retrieved along bottom as the same rate of speed as the current. As the spinner approaches the lip of the redd the fisherman allows the spinner to drop into the redd in front of the fish's nose. Usually the spinner is seized immediately (most often by the male) and the strike is made.

If the fish ignore the spinner or separate and allow the spinner to sweep through between them, lift the spinner out as soon as it passes their nose and make another cast directly upstream from the fish. Fast accurate casting is the key to making this method produce.

Strikes are seldom hard or jarring; most strikes will occur as the spinner pauses briefly. Watch for the steelhead's head to twitch sideways as he picks up the passing spinner.

Rivermouth Spinning

Tidal basins, the first pool upstream from a rivermouth, and the actual rivermouth are all hotspots for the spinfisherman. In wide expanses like this I prefer to make several casts in a fan-like manner ahead of me as I wade and then shuffle off and cast as I go. Steelhead in these areas are often moving and the angler has the choice of either standing and allowing the fish to come to him or move off in search of cruising feeding trout. The majority of fishermen prefer the latter method, which generally produces the most steelhead.

Spinfishermen congregated around a river tidal basin. When the steelhead are in, rivermouth fishing in the Great Lakes can accommodate both wading and boating fishermen. *(Ontario Ministry of Industry and Tourism photo)*

SPINNERS AND SPINNER RIGS

As important as fishing techniques are to spinner fishing, the actual choice of spinner, spinner body and blade, weight of spinner and color of blade are equally important. As a general rule, I use a spinner heavy enough to get to the bottom without split shot or pencil lead. There are times where extra weight is needed, and when this problem is encountered, there are several ways to solve it.

If I have to use split shot ahead of a spinner I try to crimp the shot on just ahead of the spinner. Some fishermen apply their split shot or pencil lead about six or eight inches up the line from the spinner. This usually results in a tangled cast, as the spinner whips around and catches the line near the weight. Attaching the weight near the spinner insures taking the lure down near bottom, without risking tangles.

When a heavier spinner is called for, I use an Eppinger (Dardevle) No Tangle Spinner. This spinner has an offset line tie of sufficient length to allow you to crimp a split shot onto the wire line tie without affecting the balance or action of the spinner. Often one split shot is all you need to take the spinner down, and this type of spinner takes on the basic qualities of both a leadhead jig and a spinner when a split shot is added.

Spinner Color and Size

Veteran steelheaders normally swear by silver-colored blades in dark dirty water and on overcast days, and either brass or copper-colored blades in clear water or on bright days. Chartreuse or fire red spinners often pay off extremely well during high water or dirty water conditions.

During periods of low, clear water many spinner fishermen touch up their spinner blades with black spray paint or a piece of black electrician's tape. This cuts down on the reflective quality of the spinner blade in shallow, clear water. Many steelhead will rush a spinner with a black blade and spook from a shinier-colored lure.

Many steelhead anglers err by, all too often, opting for the largest blades available, whereas a smaller blade will often produce more strikes. The larger spinner will actually frighten steelhead.

A dime-size spinner blade is as small as a fisherman should

go, but nickel-size is as large as is convenient to fish with. At times the very large Colorado or Indiana spinner blades will produce steelhead during periods of high and cloudy water. The larger blades produce more sound vibrations in the water and give the fish an extra signal to home in on.

The addition of a bucktail or feathered tail on your spinner hook can be important. I've known times when treble hooks dressed with red hackle or feathers will outproduce any other color combination. The majority of steelhead fishermen, however, lean toward the bare treble hooks. Bucktailed spinners rarely produce consistent catches of steelhead, although that may be because they aren't used very frequently. In deep water, the bucktail will absorb water and sink slightly deeper than a plain hooked spinner.

Over the years I've tried all types of spinners and have found the following to be consistent steelhead producers wherever they are tried: Mepps Aglia and Mepps Long, Eppinger's No Tangle, Grizzly's Colorado and Skagit Special, Luhr Jensen's Cherry Drifter Spinner and Metric, Les Davis' Bolo Spinner, Worden's Rooster Tail and Heddon's Hep Spinner.

Spinning is one of the deadliest methods of fishing, and one of the easiest steelheading methods to learn. Master these techniques, and experiment with lure size, color and casting position, and you'll find yourself catching more and more steelhead every year.

DRIFTERS

Take a popcorn-sized piece of knobby plastic, drill a hole through it and tie one or two hooks onto the line and what do you have? An Okie Drifter, that's what.

The Okie Drifter has almost revolutionized steelhead fishing on West Coast streams, and its popularity has quickly spread to the steelhead-rich Great Lakes streams. Okie's—and their many imitations—come in three or four sizes and a vast array of colors, from the conventional spawn-color to chartreuse with red spots. Oddly enough, all colors will work at times.

The Okie Drifter was made to represent a drifting piece of roe. The Okie (many fishermen call them bobbers) is hollow and somewhat buoyant and will drift just off the bottom. The buoyancy helps keep the lure from snagging on bottom. This characteristic makes it especially appealing to steelhead drift fishermen.

Bobbers are made of cork, plastic and yarn or balsa wood—all have the admirable trait of floating up off bottom. The smallest and medium-sized bobbers are most common. Steelheaders have learned that the smaller-size bobbers are often productive when the fish aren't coming to the lure well.

Okies come in a raft of colors to meet a host of varying river conditions. In muddy water conditions a bobber in fire, orange, clown (chartreuse with red spots), chartreuse, silver or gold will often produce when bumped downstream slowly in the dark water.

Very clear low-water conditions call for a smaller bobber in almost any color. I've had excellent success over the years with chartreuse, pearl, silver, gold, clown and pink crystal colors during low water conditions. A trick I've used for clear water drifter fishing is to singe a silver bobber slightly with a kitchen match. The black residue left on the silver bobber cuts down a bit on the glare.

When rivers have a medium visibility I normally go to the brighter colors such as fire, orange, chartreuse, clown, pink and silver for my drifter bodies.

Steelhead fishermen swear that when the sun is high in the sky and the water low and clear the fisherman should go to the smallest bobber available. Larger sizes can and will spook steelhead under bright sunny conditions. It pays to keep an ample supply of small-size bobbers available for these conditions.

Carrying the drifter-body type lure one step further, we arrive at winged drifter lures. These lures have built-in action in the form of wings, which cause the body to spin on a wire shaft. Examples of this type of lure are Luhr Jensen's Prism-Glo and Worden's Spin-N-Glo and Wobble-Glo. The latter two lures attract steelhead by the sound of the revolving or wobbling body.

Wobbling drifter lures of this type are particularly deadly during high, dirty water conditions so prevalent during winter months. The same color theory holds true for this lure: fish brighter, larger, colored lures in dirty water and go to smaller offerings in low, clear streams.

The lure that kicked off the drifter-type lure business back in the early 1950's was the original Cherry Bobber. This lure was shaped from a small piece of balsa wood and painted with several layers of bright red paint. The Cherry Bobber swept through the steelhead ranks like wildfire. Today's lure market features similar lures in the Cherry Drifter and Cherry Cluster by Luhr Jensen. These lures represent the original bobber or drifter body plus the added action of a spinner blade.

Drifter Rigs

The amazing thing about the drifter-type lure is its versatility. It can be fished just the way it comes out of the package, or yarn or eggs can be added as an extra enticement. Great Lakes fishermen add two or three single salmon eggs or a spawn bag (roe sack) to the hook.

Bobber or drifter-type lures are meant to be fished on or just off bottom, just like bait. To bottom-fish these lures effectively one must use sufficient weight in the form of split shot, lead cinch or a three-way swivel arrangement to take the bait to the bottom. Enough weight must be used to take the offering down but not so much that the lure becomes anchored to the bottom. It must bounce downstream naturally.

Many drifter-type lures are factory-tied on leaders that are much too long and too heavy. Many of the commercially prepared lures are tied with two hooks—one above the drifter ball and one below. This type of hooking arrangement has little advantage; many fishermen buy their drifter bodies in bulk and tie their own leaders. The majority of steelheaders favor a short shank up-turned eye hook in either a number 2, 1/0 or 2/0 size, depending on the size of the drifter ball being used. Smaller

YARN TIE

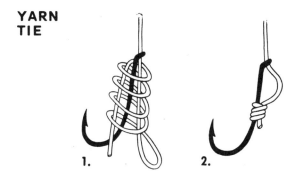

1.   2.

OKIE TIE

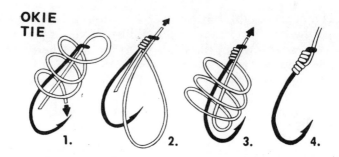

1.   2.   3.   4.

hooks, of course, are normally used with the smallest-sized drifters, or on rivers where the fish being taken are small.

Since bait or yarn is often added to the hook beneath the drifter body, it's necessary to learn to tie the proper knot to hold a piece of raw eggs or yarn. This knot is called the yarn tie and is fast and simple to learn.

Another knot used strictly with drifters is the Okie tie or bumper tie. This knot gives a direct pull on the hook point and insures proper hook setting when a fish strikes.

As effective as Okies are, I believe they can be rendered much more productive by adding a small chunk of green steelhead roe. The proper procedure is to cut a small (one inch square or smaller) chunk of roe from a partially dried skein of eggs. Eggs that haven't been dried or partially cured often fall off on the first cast.

Push the loop of monofilament up on the hook from your yarn tie and slide the roe onto the shank of the hook and pull the line tight. If the roe is green enough, cut off a piece and hook it directly onto the hook. This will often provide the most secure hooking.

The drifter now is doubly effective; it offers the color and size of the drifter ball plus the natural scent of steelhead roe. This effectiveness can be carried one step further by the addition of two or three two-inch lengths of fluorescent yarn. The yarn can either be hooked under the loop of the yarn tied hook, tied above the eye of the hook, or merely hooked or tied to the bend of the hook.

Yarn comes in a variety of colors for steelhead fishermen but I personally have found hot orange, pink, chartreuse, cerise and even white to be effective at times. Normally the hotter colors produce more strikes than cooler colors.

Fishing the Drifter

Drifters, with or without eggs and/or yarn, are fished just like bait. Cast out into the drift and allow the weight to bounce the bobber downstream in a natural manner.

Steelhead will normally strike a drifter much harder than natural bait. I've found that bait by itself produces soft delicate strikes; fish tend to take a drifter with much more power and determination. But a steelhead will gently mouth a drifter as it works downstream. This will often occur when bait is being used in conjunction with the drifter. It takes a light sensitive rod and an experienced fisherman to "read" a strike into a gentle pause. The normal reaction is to strike as soon as you feel the delicate tapping of a fish. Many times the fish is merely playing with the lure and hasn't taken the bait; if you strike when you first feel this tapping, you'll miss the fish If this occurs more than once, settle your nerves briefly by ny means, and allow the fish to mess with the bait. He'll often bunt or push it into a quiet eddy. Hold off on setting the hook until you feel a strong solid pull—then set the hook hard.

Steelheaders on the West Coast frequently make long-distance casts, with drifters, when a much shorter spot cast would enable them to detect more strikes. Fortunately, many Great Lakes streams are fairly narrow and long casts aren't necessary. But in any case, a fisherman with twenty to forty yards of line out is hard put to feel the delicate strike of a cautious steelhead. It makes much more sense to fish nearby water with drifters, and then explore the farther water once you've satisfied your curiosity about the river closest to you.

Another productive method of fishing drifters is quartering across and upstream or across and downstream. Since the lure is kept moving on a tight line, strikes are normally quite easy to detect. I discovered some years ago that a direct upstream cast with a drifter lure would enable me to fish certain areas of a river that were otherwise inaccessible to me by conventional casting methods. Now, whenever I find myself believing a steelhead to be lying in a certain hard-to-get-at spot, I'll resort to the upstream cast.

The drifter is cast at least ten to twenty feet upstream from the suspected lie and slowly worked downstream into position. You must first allow the drifter to sink to bottom and then work the lure downstream by alternately reeling slowly and raising and lowering the rod tip to take up the slack.

Strikes on the upstream cast are generally gentle affairs; set the hook anytime the drifter stops its downstream travel.

Making A Drifter

There are some fishermen who object strenuously to the price of Okies, and prefer to make their own. One variation on the Okie drifter I like to make is called the acorn drifter. Anyone with time on their hands, and a reasonable amount of skill with hand tools, can fashion enough acorn drifters in one afternoon to last a season.

The first step is to acquire a sackful of acorns. The smallest acorns should be set onto a window screen and allowed to dry thoroughly. This often takes up to a month or more depending on the climate. Once dried, drill a very small hole lengthwise through the small acorn. The acorns are then painted with various colors of lacquer and allowed to dry. Select colors that approximate those found on commercially made Okies. Once the paint is dry, they may be tied up into drifters in the same manner as a commercially produced lure. Do they work? They sure do.

Acorn drifters are simple to make and rig; the one on the right includes a yarn tie. *(Photo by the author)*

The first time I tried an acorn drifter was on a large western river. The acorn was painted up in the clown color, chartreuse with red spots. I added a couple wisps of chartreuse yarn to the hook and worked the drifter deep behind a boulder that was bulging the surface of the river.

The first pass resulted in a meek strike, which I missed. Figuring the fish wanted a bit more incentive, I added a small kernel of fresh roe. This time when the drifter floated behind the boulder I felt the savage arm-shaking strike of a big fish. That winter steelhead shot downstream with me in hot pursuit and we wrestled back and forth in waist-deep water for twenty minutes before I gently slid a 10-pound hen onto the beach. I gently unhooked her and held her upright in the water until she gained enough strength to splash off. I finished the day by hooking four other fish and landing a nice 12-pound buck which I kept. Since that day I've always carried a few acorn drifters in my fishing vest.

OTHER STEELHEADING TECHNIQUES

There are many methods of steelhead fishing that do not logically fit in any specific category. But they catch fish—and that is all that is expected of them.

My brother and I have worked out a fishing technique for spawning steelhead that is very effective. We call it "double teaming".

In Michigan, where we live, spring fishing for spawning steelhead is an accepted sport. Double teaming is a method of teasing spawning steelhead into striking. We fish for males exclusively and if a female is caught it is immediately released. The method consists of slowly stalking the river banks looking for steelhead on the redd.

Once a pair of fish, or several steelhead, are located, we work into casting position about 10 yards downstream from the fish. We pick one fish, and one fish alone, to try for. We generally single out the largest male and begin casting.

One fisherman usually uses a flyrod and reel stocked with 15-pound monofilament and a copper-bladed Mepps or Colorado spinner. The other fisherman uses either a spinning rod and reel, or a flyrod like his partner. He too uses a spinner. If the water is shallow enough, we don't use any weight ahead of the spinner. If the river is deep and swift we'll add a split shot or two about six inches ahead of the spinner.

The object is to time your casts so a spinner is passing by the male's nose at all times. One fisherman lays his spinner about ten feet upstream from the male and immediately allows it to sink as he strips line in and keeps the spinner skimming along the gravel.

The other fisherman casts just as the first man begins his retrieve. The first spinner will come past the buck's nose and as soon as it passes the fish, the fisherman lifts the spinner out and makes another cast. About the time his cast hits the water the other fisherman's spinner is teasing past the fish. This procedure is kept up until the fish strikes the twinkling lure as it sweeps through the redd.

I doubt that this method will be accepted in West Coast steelhead areas, but there is a tremendous difference between West Coast streams and those in the Great Lakes states. The various departments of natural resources also hold different opinions on what is right or wrong for their streams. I won't stand in defense of this method of fishing but merely state that it is an oddball method of steelhead fishing, one that is entirely legal where practiced, and one that produces plenty of steelhead action.

Fishing High Water

A method I call the high water "fish 'em in the woods" technique is one I learned many years ago from a renowned steelhead fishing expert, George Yontz of Wolverine, Michigan. I've since practiced this technique wherever high water conditions and steelhead exist. It worked 20 years ago and still produces fish when spring or fall freshets swell the rivers bank-full of muddy brown water.

Every steelhead fisherman has seen this type of day: the rain has been pouring down for two days, the snow or ice meltoff is in full swing and the river is over its banks and about the same color as twice-brewed coffee. Enough natural food is washing into the river to feed every trout within miles, providing the fish could hold in a feeding station long enough to eat. Unfortunately, the current is too swift and holes and runs are indistinguishable in the high water.

Where will the steelhead be in this high water, you ask? If

you know anything about steelhead you'll remember they hate to fight the full flow of the current. With a river out of its banks and running through the woods, a steelhead can't lay in the full thrust of the current for long. He's like you; he seeks comfort and this he finds in the same places where you'd normally walk along the banks.

The idea here is to put your knowledge of the riverbanks to work. Try to remember large objects that used to lie along the riverbanks, or trails that might break the flow of the heavy current. The first time I tried this trick I remembered a large granite boulder that used to lie some ten yards from the edge of the river.

The river was very high and all I could see was the tip of this large white boulder poking up through the swirling waters. I added a couple more split shot ahead of my spawn bag and drifted the bait in behind the boulder. I felt the familiar tap-tap-tap of a feeding steelhead and prodded the hook home. That fish sailed out from behind the rock and cleared the water in a thrilling head-to-tail leap. Ten minutes later I unhooked the eight pounder and released him.

Since that time I've done a good bit of experimenting with high water fishing and have found it pays to remember the large rocks, stumps, fallen trees, etc. that lay along the edge of your favorite river. These areas can become variable hotspots during high water if you use a bit of logic and forethought before fishing them.

Fishing Open Water

The open water "wade and cast" technique seems to be peculiar to the Great Lakes states, although I've seen it practiced in scattered locations along the West Coast.

Steelhead often cruise along lake shorelines in search of food prior to a spring, fall, or winter surge up the river. Summer steelhead often feed with reckless abandon in open water and the wade and cast fisherman can often hit paydirt with a bit of exploring and experimentation.

Practitioners of this sport often dress for the weather conditions and shuffle along slowly and stop every twenty yards or so and cast while standing in belly-deep water. The object is to fan out casts in a 180 degree arc around you and then move off

Fishing the open water; the splashing surf makes this Pennsylvania angler a
lonesome figure as he awaits a strike. (*Penna. Fish Commission photo*)

down the shoreline another 20-yards before stopping to cast
again.

Spinning tackle seems to be the favorite with 10 to 12-pound
test entirely adequate for both long casts and plenty of strength
to handle big fish in the surf. Spoons such as the Eppinger
Devle Dog or the Little Cleo in silver, silver-blue, hammered
silver, or crystal are deadly on these big cruising steelhead.
Spoons with silver and a red or orange slash are also top colors
for steelhead.

These fish are normally cruising in five to eight feet of water
and a wobbling spoon, with plenty of flash, seems to be the key
to obtaining strikes. It pays to experiment with the retrieve
speed and lure size and color for consistent good fishing. A

steady retrieve at the proper speed to bring out the best action of the lure is normally best.

An excellent time for wading and casting is in the spring when smelt move inshore to spawn. Steelhead will follow this food source and the fishing can be fantastic. Many times the fish can be spotted by rolling or porpoising splashes as they feed on forage fish. I've caught and released as many as thirty steelhead in a day by wading and casting.

Plunking With Plugs

An alternative plunking technique is to use a similar three-way swivel set up with a Flatfish, Tadpolly or HotShot on the end of a six to eight foot leader. This unsightly looking rig is cast out and anchored to the bottom. The long leader allows the plug to wiggle back and forth in the bottom of the hole. Plunkers trying this method for the first time should be warned to either hang onto their rod or prop it up firmly on shore to prevent a steelhead from pulling it into the river on the strike.

Steelheading With Plugs

Many anglers ignore certain so-called bass fishing techniques that can be perfectly adapted to steelhead rivers. One of the best techniques steelheaders could borrow from bass men is the use of deep-diving plugs. Heddon's Tiny Deep Diving River Runt Spook is probably the most effective lure of its type. This plug has a large metal lip designed to take it deep, provide the fish attracting wiggle and to prevent hangups in underwater brush.

The fisherman, in either boat or wading, should position himself straight across from a suspected steelhead lie. Cast the plug quartering across and upstream. Keep the rod tip low to the water and reel just fast enough to bring out the wiggle of the plug.

Retrieve the lure down through the depths of a hole. This technique works well in deep resting pools where other methods seldom pay off. If the downstream travel of the lure stops, set the hook. Surprisingly enough, a steelhead seldom hits this lure with a bang. It just stops as though snagged on bottom.

The best steelhead colors are perch scale, red head with

white body and black and white shore minnow. The yellow coachdog color is also productive at times.

Jigging

Another bass fishing technique that works well on deeper rivers is jig fishing. I prefer jigs in the ¼ to ½-ounce sizes and the Gapen Pinky jig is one of my favorites. I use Pinky's in red, yellow or white, or if the need arises, I switch to an Ugly Bug in brown or black. Darker-colored jigs produce well in dark muddy water while the brighter jigs will produce at almost any time of year or under any water condition.

The best method of fishing jigs is to cast quartering across and upstream. Allow the jig to reach bottom and then work it slowly downstream with short hippety-hop movements of the rod tip. Keep the rod fairly low (at a 9 o'clock position) and raise the rod tip sharply about two feet and then allow the jig to sink to bottom. Reel up the slack line as it works downstream and following each jigging movement of the rod tip.

Steelhead usually take the jig just as it settles into a new area. Strikes can be rather soft but they often are forceful and an angler has no trouble telling he's had a strike.

Some steelhead streams have large amounts of crayfish present and many fish feed on this bait. A brownish colored jig with brown bucktail is often a deadly combination for this situation.

Some jig fishermen steal a page from the walleye fisherman's tactics. Try attaching a tiny sliver of fish flesh or belly strip to a jig. The extra scent or flutter of the strip often causes a prowling steelhead to home in on the jig.

Minnow Fishing

Minnow fishing is a method of steelhead fishing many anglers have never tried. A minnow sewed onto a hook is one of the most deadly methods devised for river fishing. Select an inch-and-a-half to two-inch minnow (shiner). Be sure to select a fresh minnow, and not one that has been dead and floating in the minnow bucket for hours. Thread the hook through the minnow's mouth, out its gills and hook the point into the side of the minnow. The minnow will hang straight on the line and look natural in the water. Fish the minnow in the same manner as

A jig-hooked steelhead comes to the surface. *(Photo by the author)*

any type of bait. Steelhead will often strike the minnow hard enough to hook themselves.

Sometimes steelhead strike minnows across the body and fail to become hooked. If this happens, attach a second hook further up the line and fasten this second hook through the minnow's lips. This normally solves the problem of short-striking steelhead.

"Mono Fishing"

An interesting variation on the flyfishing theme has been developed recently on certain Michigan rivers. Many of these steelhead goldmines are so choked with logjams and brushpiles that conventional flyfishing is out of the question. Fishermen who still wish to fish with flies spool level monofilament onto their fly reels and fish streamers, wets and nymphs just like bait.

One, two or three split shot are crimped onto the mono about six to twelve inches above the fly. Since casting space puts conventional flyfishing out of the question, this new breed of steelheader uses a soft pendulum or lob cast to place the fly in the proper place. The split shot enables the fisherman to fish into tight quarters where a conventional fly could never go. The fly and split shot is lobbed upstream from the suspected lie and allowed to bounce downstream in a natural manner. The rod tip is kept at about 10 o'clock position and whenever the fly stops, set the hook. Steelhead often take a fly presented in this manner in a very delicate manner. Normally the fly just stops its downstream journey and that's the time to set the hook. This method of "mono fishing" a fly has opened the doors for many fishermen to take steelhead on a fly. Some spin fishermen have also adopted this method of fly fishing.

Oddball techniques are sometimes the only avenue left open to steelhead fishermen when conventional tactics fail to produce. Try these tricks when you find your normal technique failing and it may produce a banner fishing day for you.

Boating Techniques
For Steelhead

Two spectacular fishing methods have evolved for boating steelheaders; the dropback method, a Great Lakes innovation, and hot-shotting, a technique favored by West Coast fishermen. These methods are quite similar in the lure's approach to the fish, but drastically different in execution. Much of the success of either method lies in being able to read the river. A quick course of reading a deep river: fish any deep water runs along the edges of the riverbanks. Steelhead often lay close to the riverbank, or just behind or alongside a logjam or sweeper, and will smack a lure being dropped back through their holding spot. Pools and fast runs with moderately deep water (eight to fifteen feet) just below a gravel bar are often productive. Spots like this are hot during spring months as steelhead migrate upstream to spawn. The fish often take refuge in the first deep hole or run just below a gravel bar to rest up between bouts on the spawning redds.

Other deep river hotspots are to be found directly below obstructions, such as a large boulder or deadhead in the river that breaks up the current flow. Steelhead will seek out small pockets of quiet water such as this, and the steelheader should never pass them up.

The first drift or deep run downstream from a stream flowing into the main river should be fished thoroughly. Steelhead will spend some time at these locations, before moving up the smaller fork.

DROPBACK FISHING

Dropback fishing is done from an anchored, motionless boat. Hotshotting is done from a drift boat that is slowly and carefully rowed and drifted through the best holding water while the angler fishes with just a set amount of line out behind the boat.

Two lures do yeoman duty for the dropback fisherman. A U-20 Flatfish or a medium-sized Heddon Tadpolly are the best choices. The Flatfish is used strictly in low water conditions when the current isn't too strong. Too much current will cause the Flatfish to turn and come to the surface, but during low water conditions, the wiggling effect of this type of lure drives steelhead wild.

The Tadpolly is better suited to high, fast water conditions. This lure will dive deeply with a vigorous wiggle during high water and will not surface under heavy current flow conditions. Both lures are often used interchangeably during any given day on the river.

Lure color seems to be important and the Redhead Flitter, Spotted Orange and silver to be the best colors for Tadpollys while silver, grey pearl, orange with black stripe, and embossed scale gold-plated Flatfish produce the majority of strikes.

Reading of the river is essential in dropback fishing, but boat placement is equally important. The boat must be anchored directly upstream from the suspected steelhead lie. Five feet one way or the other can spell the difference between success and failure in this type of fishing.

Once the boat is properly anchored about 20 or 30 yards upstream from where the fish are located, the rods and reels are readied with either a Flatfish or Tadpolly, depending on the water conditions. I recommend an 8½ to 9-foot baitcasting rod with a free spool level-wind baitcasting reel spooled with 20-pound braided Dacron.

Lower the lure over the edge of the riverboat and pay out twenty feet of line initially. Keep firm thumb pressure on the reel arbor and allow the lure to wiggle seductively in the current on a tight line.

After the plug has done its wiggling bit for fifteen to thirty seconds in one spot, raise your thumb slightly and allow another three feet of line to slide out downstream. Apply thumb pressure again and allow the lure to wiggle in its new location. After the plug works like this for another fifteen to thirty seconds, release three more feet of line and stop the plug again. The lure, in this stop and go manner, is "dropped back" downstream three feet at a time until the entire drift has been covered. A lure should be worked for up to one minute in each location during extremely cold water periods.

The maximum length of a dropback run should be seventy-five to one hundred yards. If the run is longer than that, lift the anchor and drop downstream seventy-five yards and make another set. Anchor and use the dropback method until the entire run has been fished thoroughly.

The majority of the strikes will come just as the plug drops back into its new location. Steelhead react in one of three manners when they see a lure dropping gradually down to them: they'll either spook, move out of the way of the intruder, or smack the plug viciously. When a steelhead does strike on a drop back plug, it hits like dynamite. Always maintain a firm grip on the rod, holding it horizontally over the edge of the boat. Many rods have been lost over the side of the boat.

A dropback trick that often works is to swing the rod horizontally across the stern of the boat. This will cause the plug to travel as much as ten feet across the river from its original location, and a steelhead will often hit the plug as it swings across the current. Another trick that sometimes produces is to abruptly raise your rod tip to a vertical position. This will cause the plug to increase its vibrating wiggle and will occasionally trigger a strike.

This method of steelhead fishing is a consistent producer of large fish. It seldom produces small steelhead; the majority of fish taken will usually run at least ten pounds or larger.

If a large fish is struck on a long line it is important to quickly raise the anchor and drift down on the fish before it gains any slack line and dives into brush or nearby logjams. Many steelhead will run upstream toward the boat as soon as they feel the barbs. It is very important to reel quickly and gain a tight line before the steelhead has the opportunity to jump and throw the plug.

HOTSHOTTING

Hotshotting is quite common to Oregon and Washington streams such as the Rogue, Cowlitz, Skagit, Bogachiel, Hoh, Sol Duc and the Calawah. A drift boat of the McKenzie or Rogue River type is the most common hotshotting boat. These rivers are often comprised of white water haystacks standing around the large boulders dotting the streams. Steelhead lurk around these obstructions, and the successful hotshotter is in for a thrilling strike and fast action in this swift water.

Hotshotting is one of the easiest methods of steelhead fishing to master. Normally two fishermen sit in the stern of a drift boat as the fishing guide allows the boat to slowly drift downstream.

Some fishermen prefer baitcasting outfits for hotshotting although a growing number of steelheaders are leaning to open face spinning outfits.

The HotShot is also a plug which has gained wide acclaim on the West Coast streams for producing large steelheads. It has a fast-wiggling movement that dives to depths of five to eight feet and it comes in a variety of fish-catching colors. Some of the favorites of hotshotters are silver, pink pearl, luminescent, and chartreuse.

Let out about forty or fifty feet of line from the spinning or baitcasting reel and allow the HotShot to work ahead of the boat. The lure will float on the surface ahead of the boat until the guide begins rowing upstream. The guide knows the best water and he positions the HotShot in the proper place before rowing against the current.

The lure will dive toward bottom and swing back and forth in the current as the boat drifts downstream. Once a lure has worked through the lie once, the guide will often re-position the boat upstream from the steelhead lie and allow the boat and lure to work through the run again.

The drift boat is an efficient machine; a quick stroke with one oar is usually sufficient to swing the boat several feet into more productive water. The man with the rod has little to do with the actual fishing of the lure. He merely holds onto the rod and makes sure the tip is working correctly. The guide does all the work in positioning the lure over productive water.

The same basic sections of a stream produce for hotshotters as for the dropback fishermen. The hotshotter normally is able to fish water either overlooked by other steelheaders, or inaccessible to bank or wading fishermen because of snags or other bottom debris. This type of fishing requires no weight to take the lure near bottom. The plugs, with their elongated lips, dive quite easily in moderate to heavy currents, and they're relatively resistant to snagging on underwater obstructions.

Some fishermen argue that dropback and hotshot lures spook all the steelhead from the lies. This theory has been proven wrong many times and has no basis in fact. A good drift fisherman can often come along right behind a hotshotter or dropback fisherman and catch steelhead with other lures or bait. These two methods of steelhead fishing can be very productive under the proper circumstances and should be considered two secret weapons in the steelheader's bag of tricks.

STEELHEAD RIVER BOATS

Steelhead boats vary in size and shape, but all of them are geared to suit the moods of particular rivers.

There are basically four different types of boats for steelheading: the McKenzie drift boat, the Rogue River drift boat, heated and cabined steelheading boats, and small cartop aluminum boats suitable for slow water and estuaries.

There are many variations of drift boats found in the Pacific Northwest. Every boatbuilder or private drift boat fisherman has his idea as to what constitutes a good drift boat and these characteristics are often built into the boat by the owner. Drift boats are made to slide effortlessly through white water, rapids, over and around water-bulging rocks, and through fast chutes without shipping water.

Drift boats are made of marine plywood, fiberglass or aluminum. Of the three, aluminum is usually the most popular, since it requires little maintenance. Fiberglass hulls are racy looking and hold up well but are generally much heavier. Drift boats are made for one-way travel—downstream; a boat trailer must be waiting at the other end to take the boat out.

A drift boat on the Skagit. *(Photo by the author)*

Drift Boats

The McKenzie River boat was designed for use on the swift McKenzie River. This type of boat is light and has plenty of freeboard. It's designed to drift downstream stern first with the guide easing the boat through likely steelhead lies by rowing with or against the current. Two men is about all the McKenzie River boat can handle: one fisherman leaning against the transom and the guide in the bow on the oars.

The Rogue River drift boat is wider in the beam than the narrower McKenzie boat; two or three fishermen, as well as the guide, can sit comfortably. The stern rises sharply out of the water, which prevents rushing water from catching on the stern and swiveling the craft about in the current. A hard pull on one oar will sideslip the boat around a protruding boulder or prolonged rowing can hold the craft stationary at the lip of a roaring riffle while the fishermen drift their lures or bait through the best holding water.

A small three-to-six horsepower motor can be attached to a Rogue River drift boat for convenience in cruising at hull speed through slow calm stretches of river where the majority of drift boat guides never fish.

Rogue River drift boats float downstream bow-first. The fishermen sit in a forward seat and face their baits at all times. The oarsman faces forward and rows backward and thus remains in control of the drift boat at all times.

The Jet Sled

A rather new variation of the drift boat is the jet sled. This craft is usually about twenty feet long and powered by an inboard-outboard jet. Jet sleds are capable of going either up or downstream, a big advantage to steelheaders; once a jet sledder finds a school of fish he can stay with them instead of drifting slowly past and getting only one shot at the fish. Jet sleds are also capable of taking more fishermen per trip and they are becoming increasingly popular with western steelhead guides.

Cabined Boats

The heated river boat is becoming very popular in Michigan, where winter steelheading is a cold but productive sport. Capt. Emil Dean of Bear Lake, Michigan introduced the first heated and cabined river boat on the Big Manistee River several years ago. The boat is an 18-foot John boat with an aluminum cabin constructed so fishermen (usually two) and the guide can sit inside, out of the wintry blasts and enjoy a warming cup of coffee, or even a hot meal cooked on a bottled gas stove.

The heated river boat is normally powered by a fifty or sixty-horsepower outboard engine equipped with power tilt to raise or lower the engine over deadheads and other debris from the timbering era of a century ago.

An electric winch is used on the bow of the heated river boat to raise or lower the forty-pound ball of chains that serves as an anchor. Chains are used because they are the only anchor that will not snag or catch in the submerged logs and treetops found on many Michigan rivers.

Two deck chairs sit outside the cabin and the fishermen work from these chairs. Rolling spawn bags through deep drifts or dropback fishing Flatfish or Tadpollies are the two top methods of fishing from this type of river boat.

Cabined riverboats have caught on on many remote Ontario steelhead streams, and some anglers are using this boat as a sort of base of operations. They can cook, eat, sleep and fish aboard the boat in pristine wilderness along any one of a hundred steelhead streams flowing into the north shore of Lake Superior.

Cartop Boats

The small aluminum cartop boat in the ten to twelve-foot size is entirely adequate for floating to steelhead hotspots in tidal

This cabined, heated riverboat will keep these two anglers warm and comfortable even on an overnight steelheading expedition. *(Photo by the author)*

estuaries, and for certain slow moving streams. A craft of this type is *not* suited to negotiating rapid streams, because it doesn't have the maneuverability of boats like the McKenzie or Rogue River models.

Cartoppers are most suitable for the slower-moving portions of lower rivers. Many of the West's great steelhead streams are paralleled by highways and a small cartop boat can be easily transported by one or two fishermen down the bank and into the river. A small kicker can be used to push the light boat back upstream to the car at the end of a day of fishing.

Cartop and small trailerable boats are in wide use in many of the Midwest's small inland lakes, where migrating steelhead from the Great Lakes pause before shooting up the spawning streams. Trolling is the popular means of fishing these lakes and a small boat and motor makes this an interesting and productive way to fish. Access sites and good ramps allow trailered boats easy access to the best steelhead water.

Most driftboats have a great deal of freeboard which makes for a safe dry ride through rough water. The heated riverboat also has ample freeboard for safety afloat. But high-sided boats make netting a hazardous proposition, unless the craft is outfitted with a long-handled net.

Many steelhead fisherman prefer to anchor and cast to particular drifts. An electric winch can raise and lower the anchor if it weighs over twenty pounds.

Boating Tactics

Fighting a steelhead from a boat calls for cooperation between the guide and his customer, or between two fishermen. We've all been advised that a fisherman should never stand up in a boat, but, providing the fisherman is calm and careful, he will often find it to his advantage. I always stand up in the boat when I have a fish on because it allows for better control over the fish. I can anticipate changes in direction sooner and can cope with sudden lunges or jumps. For the same reason, I heartily advocate the use of life preservers when fishing from a boat. I prefer the wearable vests which are produced by Stearns in a vast assortment of colors and styles. A fisherman wearing a life preserver has more confidence in his ability to land fish because he doesn't have that nagging fear of falling overboard.

When hooked from a boat, steelhead often either dash off

downstream in a headlong flight coupled with water-shattering jumps, or they charge upstream past the boat. The steelheader must be able to cope with either reaction. If you're anchored in midstream or along the edge of a drift and your steelhead heads downstream, follow the fish, if the run takes out more than 50 yards of line. Keep as close to the steelhead as possible. Remember to keep the rod tip high, the drag properly set, and your hands off the spool. More steelhead are lost because of improperly set drags and heavy thumbs on spool arbors than for any other reason.

When the fish takes off, lift the anchor quickly and allow the boat to drift silently down onto the fish while the angler keeps the line tight. Once you've caught up to the fish, drop the anchor and begin playing the steelhead again. Always be prepared to raise the anchor quickly if the steelhead runs toward the boat. This may prevent the fish from fouling the line on the anchor line.

If a fish is hooked and runs upstream from your anchored boat, the best procedure is to remain anchored and allow the fish to fight both the current and the rod pressure. It doesn't take too much of this kind of effort to make most steelhead turn tail and head downstream. When a steelie swaps ends and heads downstream, he can do so with great speed; be prepared for this tactic, and if necessary, raise the anchor and follow the fish.

Boondoggling

"Boondoggling" is a practice as familiar to steelheading as it is in the halls of Congress. The name is the same but the fishing technique is more productive. This steelheading tactic is practiced heavily on some Washington rivers such as the Skagit. The Skagit carries such a volume of boat traffic that a system was developed to give all fishermen a chance at the more productive drifts on the river—called "boondoggling".

The boat fishermen will drift down through the run, fishing as they go, and then turn around and run upstream for another go at the drift, especially if it holds fish. Some fisherman prefer to run a stretch of river four or five times to assure themselves there are no fish present.

Additional weight is generally needed to keep the bait or lure near bottom as the drift is made. When the drift is completed, the fisherman reels up his offering and either motors back upstream for another drift or moves off to try a more productive location. A cast and retrieve method seems to produce the majority of strikes although some fishermen prefer to drift a Spin-N-Glo behind the boat as it slides downstream.

TROLLING FOR STEELHEAD

We had just rounded a point in Michigan's Manistee Lake when suddenly the starboard rod jerked toward the lake's surface, and far astern a huge steelhead hung momentarily in the cold December sun before splashing mightily back into the lake. Seconds later the water erupted again as the fish vaulted into the air with gill covers flared wide and red, water dripping from the fish's head like tiny droplets of rain.

The steelhead sounded toward the lake bottom with a line-grabbing run. Fifteen minutes later the fight was still on, as the steelhead yawed back and forth off the stern with mighty surges of its powerful tail. Finally the fish allowed itself to be led toward the waiting net.

The steelhead, a gleaming silver buck fresh from Lake Michigan, later scaled nineteen and one-half pounds on proven scales. Three other mint-silver steelies from twelve and one-half to sixteen and one-half pounds made it a profitable day of late-season trolling.

It seems odd that more steelhead fishermen haven't discovered the fine art of trolling. Perhaps it's because when steelhead trolling hits its peak, the winter drift fishermen are doing their thing, and this exciting brand of steelhead fishing is all but forgotten.

Trolling, to some greenhorn steelheaders, means simply riding around in a boat with lures over the side. This impression is far from the truth; the dedicated steelhead troller pays as much attention to his lures and method of fishing as does the lure or fly fisherman.

Trolling Boats

The boat one uses for trolling can range from a small pram or johnboat capable of being carried from the car and over tidal bars to larger fiberglass cruisers suitable for launching from deepwater ramps. The size of the boat isn't nearly as important as how it performs at the critical slow trolling speeds.

Trolling boats should be vibration-free. Vibrations from a boat cavitating at slow speeds, shimmying engine mounts and oar-locks will spook steelhead. Many trollers shy away from any means of propulsion except rowing. They argue *any* engine noise is bound to spook fish, so they resort to arm power. A stout man on the oars will catch as many or more steelhead than will any man with a small outboard, with the possible exception of the fisherman who uses an electric trolling motor.

A sonar unit is a trolling necessity. Steelhead favor underwa-ter structure such as dropoffs, points, submerged pilings, sandbars and the like, and a common trolling pattern would normally follow a dropoff or breakline along a weedbed or sandbar or the dropoff along both sides of a point. These breaks in underwater structure often are found in the eight to fifteen-foot depths, although steelhead will often follow this type of structure in the twenty-foot depths as well.

Normally steelhead can be seen cruising in this shallower range on the sonar unit. Migrating steelhead often reveal their presence in a lake or estuary by rolling or porpoising and vet-eran trollers zero in on steelhead by glassing for rolling fish. Often porpoising steelhead will travel in schools of fifty to one hundred fish. Surfacing steelhead will seldom strike although those fish found below porpoising steelhead will. It pays to be alert to rolling fish and to troll in the immediate vicinity.

Trolling is a slow motion sport. In fact, it is impossible to troll too slow. Lake steelhead seem to cruise up from bottom and follow a slowly wiggling plug for great distances before the ac-tual strike occurs.

Trolling Tackle.

Trolling for steelhead is a sport designed for either light ac-tion spinning or baitcasting outfits. Ten to twelve-pound monofilament offers enough strength to fight big steelhead, and is still not too heavy for these leader-shy fish.

A multitude of lures will work for steelhead but they all must produce a seductive side-to-side wiggle at super-slow trolling speeds. For this reason I use a Flatfish for medium-to-shallow depth trolling and a new lure called the Ping-A-T for deep water trolling. Both lures have a violent wiggle at slow speeds, and each is designed to fish effectively at various depths.

The Flatfish works the best (I use it 90 percent of the time) at depths of fifteen feet or less. Over the years I've found Flatfish in X4, X5 and U20 are the best trolling sizes for steelhead. The Ping-A-T is made in two sizes, and the smaller version should be deadly on steelhead in ten to fifteen feet of water. The larger Ping-A-T is effective down to the 20-foot depths.

At certain times steelhead will frequent the shallows. When the fish work into four to eight feet of water the best choice of lures is an SPU or SPS Flatfish.

The productive colors seem to change on a daily basis although chrome, grey pearl, orange with black stripe, silver with pink spots, and fluorescent red with black spots are the all-around steady producers. It pays to experiment with lure size and color. I normally will pull two different colors of the same size lure for an hour. If this fails to produce a strike, I switch colors and go either one size larger or smaller. Normally a smaller lure will produce more firmly-hooked strikes than a larger lure. The fish tend to take smaller lures deeper into their mouths where a larger lure is often struck from the side and the fish is often hooked with just one hook.

I've found that, in dirty water, a darker-colored lure will produce many more strikes than a brightly colored plug. Bear this in mind if you are fishing after a heavy rain.

Trolling Tactics

There seems to be a direct correlation between time of day and peak fishing activity: early morning and just before dark have traditionally proved to be the hottest periods for trolling. Another hot time generally occurs around noon when many fishermen are heading in to eat. The troller that sticks it out during the lunch hour often finds himself locked up with a brawling steelhead while the others are winding cold fingers around hot cups of coffee.

Trolling during November and December is a cold, rugged sport and strikes seem to materialize at the oddest moments. I've known times when strikes were conspicuous by their absence during periods of heavy cloud cover; let the sun peek through for a few minutes and steelhead will often go on the prod. During periods of changing light conditions, it pays to pull lures of the same size, but with one darker colored lure for dark weather conditions and a silver or brightly colored plug for periods when the sun comes out.

Steelhead trolling is basically a longline affair. Flatfish are normally pulled about seventy-five to one hundred yards behind the slow moving boat. The lures are run out slowly from the boat as it trolls along and particular attention must be paid to prevent the lures from tangling with each other or with their own line. I prefer to tie the monofilament directly to the line tie without benefit of a swivel. If a swivel must be used, keep it as small as possible so as to prevent hindering the crucial action of the lure.

Once the lines are set, it's possible to either place the rods in rodholders or hold onto them; I much prefer to hold onto the rods, so I can feel the power of the strike. The drags must be set fairly loose to avoid a broken line on the strike.

The boat operator flips on the sonar unit and follows the contour of the shore in the eight to fifteen-foot depth. He watches both ahead and to all sides for signs of rolling fish and also watches the sonar units for "blips" of cruising fish beneath the boat. Steelhead will often cruise out from under the boat and never be marked on the sonar unit. This is the reason why the lures are trolled so far behind the boat; the fish will spook from beneath the boat but will cruise back to their original position after the boat passes and be in line to intercept the lures when they come by.

Over the years several types of structure have proven to be select places in which to find steelhead. One of the hottest is the largest hole off the mouth of a steelhead river. This could be either a large hole at the rivermouth, a tidal basin where fresh and brackish water mix and where steelhead congregate before pressing on upstream, or it could be a deep hole as much as a half-mile away from the mouth of the river.

Trolling is quite easy fishing since the angler can quickly tell if his lure is working properly or not. If the rod tip pulsates with a vibrant beat the lure is doing its job far behind the boat. If the rod tip bends over toward the water or ceases its throbbing beat then it is possible you've picked up a leaf or some other type of debris on the line or lure.

A trick that often works if you elect to hand hold your rod is to slowly sweep it forward toward the bow of the boat. This speeds up the wiggle of the lure and a following fish often picks this time to unload all over the plug. But never sweep the rod so far forward that you can't set the hook.

A zigzag trolling pattern as you follow the contour of the dropoff is another useful trolling trick. The zigzag pattern will move your lures through water the boat hasn't passed over and this will often spell the difference between success and failure on a hard day on the water. Make small zigs and zags of only ten to twenty feet. This is sufficient to cause the lures to dart and change direction quickly. Following steelhead will often strike just as the lure changes direction.

Another trolling trick that often pays off occasionally is speeding up the engine for ten or fifteen feet. This sudden brief surge of power will increase the tempo of the lure and a trailing fish will often strike out of reflex at a lure it feels is trying to get away.

Steelhead trollers have found that fish often will strike best as the boat goes into a turn or curves around a dropoff. This striking as a boat turns has prompted many trollers to make sudden turns or changes of direction in an attempt to increase the number of strikes. The turning seems to produce best when made directly off a rivermouth or other natural gathering location for steelhead.

Lastly, trolling is a method that rarely produces small fish. The average size steelhead taken trolling will be on the high side of ten pounds and twenty-pound fish aren't uncommon.

There is something decidedly unpleasant yet soul-satisfying to set out an early winter storm on a tidal basin or Great Lakes inland lake and troll for steelhead. The suspense of the unknown is always present; trolling always produces some of the largest steelhead taken each year and no one knows whether the next drag-sizzling strike will be a record fish or not. That's what brings the steelhead trollers out every year for their own special brand of self-inflicted punishment. One slashing strike, a hard fought battle with one or two head-strong leaps and all the misery has been worth it.

Boat fishing for steelhead can extend an angler's steelheading virtually to all seasons. With a properly equipped boat he can fish early migrating steelhead as they cross the sandbars from the ocean and pause in tidal lagoons; he can fish inland lakes; drift a whitewater river; fish in comfort in below zero temperature; or live aboard a boat in a life of simple luxury along some remote Canadian steelhead stream. No other form of steelheading offers the fisherman such a choice of fishing activities.

Storied Steelhead Streams West

A "storied" steelhead stream is a special river, spoken of reverently by anglers congregated at tackle shops and around secluded campfires. Qualifications for a storied stream are simple. It must be a river around which much of our steelhead heritage has grown; it must have survived the ravages of man and nature; it must be a consistent steelhead producer, year after year; and last but not least, it must have that special magic quality that captures the heart and soul of a steelheader.

There are hundreds of rivers in the United States and Canada that host steelhead runs but precious few of them have thoroughly "captured" their anglers.

Streams of this caliber have contributed significantly to the relatively new sport of steelheading. Much of the lore of a storied stream revolves around famous pools, renowned fishermen or huge runs of giant steelhead, or rivers that flow smooth and easy through towering stands of redwood.

Undoubtedly the premier Western steelhead stream is Oregon's Rogue River. Zane Grey immortalized this river in his many works which were written at Winkle Bar. Grey fished the river often and became a well-known angler on the Rogue and the nearby North Umpqua.

The Rogue River slices across Oregon's Coastal Range and the stretch of river between Grants Pass and Gold Beach, along the Pacific Coast, is acknowledged to be some of the finest steelhead water available to fishermen. Anglers come from around the world to fish this hallowed and productive water. Local flies were devised to suit existing conditions, and the Rogue has come to be the standard of any angler's ability to consistently take steelhead.

The Stillaguamish River in Washington is another river that has stood the test of time, and emerged as one of the finest and steadiest producers of steelhead. The "Stilly" hosts a fine run of summer steelhead, and the North Fork enjoys a "flies only" status that befits these summer run fish. Deer Creek, a tributary of the Stillaguamish, was producing excellent steelhead for those anglers willing to work for them during the 1915 to 1920 era. Legends of Deer Creek steelhead are still spoken of in hushed tones although few anglers are still alive that were able to cash in on this early steelhead bonanza. Deer Creek still produces steelhead but siltation is now a problem, especially after heavy rains.

Washington's Skagit River between Sedro Woolley and Rockport is probably the number one steelhead-producing river along the Pacific Coast. The Skagit is a large boating-sized river with several launches between the two towns. Steelhead taken from the Skagit rank among some of the largest taken from American West Coast waters, and 20-pound fish are not uncommon. A fine paved road parallels the Skagit for miles and makes it easily accessible for today's traveling fishermen.

The Eel River in California also has a glowing reputation for producing some of the largest steelhead taken along the Pacific shoreline. Sportsmen have made angling pilgrimages to the Eel for three-quarters of a century and have reveled in catching big steelhead amid beautiful surroundings. The Eel isn't quite as highly rated a stream as it once was but enough big fish are still caught to make this lengthy river system one of the finest steelhead streams available to anglers today.

British Columbia is just beginning to be discovered by serious steelhead fishermen. True, some adventuresome anglers made treks into B.C. for steelhead for the last 20 to 30 years but to date most of the fishing has been concentrated around just a few rivers.

The Kispiox has justifiably earned the reputation of being the best steelhead stream in the world. Flyfishermen flock to this river every year during September and October for a bout with some of the world's largest steelhead.

The Kispiox has many small feeder streams as its headwaters and as a result is often high and dirty. This factor, and its relative inaccessibility, accounts for a rather hit or miss affair on this fine river. Catch the Kispiox during low water and you'll be hard put to find a lovelier river with its stretches of fast water, deep pools, and shallow bars.

Steelhead taken from the Kispiox are generally a much thicker and heavier fish than those taken from many other streams. The bulk of the Kispiox fish arrive in September and October in a sexually mature condition. Twenty pound steelhead are not uncommon and fish up to and over thirty pounds are taken every fall. Flyfishing for steelhead is the accepted method of taking Kispiox steelhead although spinfishermen take large numbers of big fish from this and other nearby rivers in the Sheena River system.

There are many other small and reasonably inaccessible streams in British Columbia that undoubtedly host runs of giant steelhead like the Kispiox. As more and more of British Columbia is opened up, and as anglers prospect new rivers for steelhead, these new hotspots will be discovered.

WEST COAST STREAMS

Fishing offers many variables and steelhead fishing on the West Coast is a case in point; some streams support only winter runs of fish while others have some steelhead in them on an almost yearly basis. Some rivers remain largely unaffected by rainfall; a heavy dew on the morning grass will put certain others high, roily and over the banks. Streams like this are unfishable for two to five days. The Pacific Coast angler has many problems to face—some that are seldom or never faced by his Great Lakes counterpart. Whereas many Great Lakes streams are within just a few miles of each other, a steelhead fisherman on the West Coast often must cross miles of redwood-clad mountains to find another fishable stream during periods of heavy winter rains.

Steelhead range all the way from San Francisco Bay on the south to Alaska's cold arctic water. British Columbia and Alaska both have many untapped streams, where steelhead runs exist and fishing pressure is almost non-existent.

This chapter on where to fish for steelhead along the West Coast will be devoted solely to the more well-known streams. The advanced steelheader will already have his favorite locations, or be willing to search out new hotspots. The novice fisherman will be much more interested in learning about the already productive locations.

There are upwards of five hundred fishable steelhead streams in the California, Oregon, Washington, Idaho, British Columbia and Alaska area and all of them can provide from good to excellent fishing at various times of the year. The smart steelheader learns the characteristics of two or three good rivers and spends most of his time on them. The advantages of doing this are many; first of all, he knows the streams and where fish hold at all times of the year. Secondly, since he knows the rivers intimately, he'll know when to avoid them or when to fish them, according to the prevailing weather. He will not plan a steelhead trip only to find the river out of its banks due to an unexpected rainfall. The veteran steelheader knows a backup stream where rain doesn't unduly affect the water flow, and he still can make his trip.

Prospecting for steelhead in new rivers is certainly a great deal of fun but it should be done only after you've learned how to fish other, nearby rivers.

Maps pinpoint access sites, and in many cases, major highways that run parallel to the stream flow, so that anglers can drive from one good spot to another with a minimum amount of delay. Much of the Northwest's land is owned by the state and steelheaders seldom need to seek permission to cross private land to the water. This chapter will note those normally dependable streams in the Pacific Northwest that host runs of steelhead. Listed will be the closest towns, when to fish, license fees and other information.

CALIFORNIA

Steelhead enter rivers roughly from San Francisco north, although there are several rivers south of San Francisco which afford a mediocre brand of steelheading. Many of California's rivers are fished extremely hard due to their close proximity to major metropolitan areas. Fishermen can drive to steelhead rivers north of San Francisco in just a matter of a few hours. Consequently, some rivers are fished so heavily that veteran steelheaders often ignore the big name streams and concentrate their efforts on some of the lesser-known California steelhead rivers.

California resident license fees are $4.00; non-resident $15.00; 10-day non-resident $5.00; trout and salmon license stamps $3.00. Other steelhead information can be obtained by writing State of California, Dept. of Fish and Game, 1416 Ninth Street, Sacramento, CA 95814.

Eel River - This is a favorite river among California steelheaders because it produces some very large fish (some fish up to twenty pounds). The current isn't nearly as strong in the Eel as in many other West Coast streams. The best fishing normally occurs from October through January. A boat is needed for fishing near the rivermouth. Some excellent flyfishing is available when the water runs clear between rains. It is located off US 101 near Fortuna.

Garcia River - A very lightly fished river at its best during December although some fish are taken both earlier and later. Some very large fish are taken from the tidewater areas. Some excellent fishing is located upstream. Pays to investigate this river. Highway 1 near Pt. Arena.

Klamath River - This world-famous steelhead river enjoys excellent fishing from early fall (September) through the rainy season of December and January. The lower portion of the river is normally fished from boats although plunkers and drift fishermen ply select locations. The upper portion of the river is considered superior flyfishing water by veteran fishermen. The runs usually peak during October and November. A good river for lots of steelhead with the occasional trophy sized fish up to twenty pounds. Smaller eight to ten-pounders are much more common. Located near Klamath on US 101 for the lower river and Orleans on Highway 96 on the upper river. One of the top rivers along the West Coast.

Mattole River - This is a small river, as West Coast rivers go, and the tidal bar must be washed out by rain and high water before the fish can make their push upstream. Usually offers its best fishing after November. This is a lightly fished river and it can be a bit difficult for the average steelheader to get to and fish. The best bet to reach the river is to follow highway 36 to Petrolia.

Redwood Creek - The word creek is a misnomer; the river is a big river although short in length. It has big runs of large fish and isn't fished as extensively as some of the others. It flows through Redwood National Park near Orick on US 101.

Russian River - This is an excellent winter stream. The river normally is very productive during January and February although the runs can begin in December with heavy rainfall. The Russian receives a heavy fishing pressure along its entire length. Some of the river is best fished by boat. A popular Pacific Coast river that pays off with good fishing—although a bit crowded at times. The lower Russian is fished near Jenner on Highway 1 and the upper river near Healdsburg on US 101.

Smith River - This river in northern California is known as a producer of very big steelhead. It provides good steelhead fishing from October to February with a peak occurring sometime around Christmas to New Years. The Smith is one of the fastest clearing streams in the Pacific Northwest and this is one reason why the river is in such favor with anglers. Best fishing occurs near Crescent City along US 101. A highly rated California river.

Trinity River - A well-known river for winter steelhead. It hits its peak from November through January. Best fishing occurs in the Willow Creek-Salyer area along Highway 299. Indian guides are available in the Hoopa area of Highway 96. Some big fish are taken each winter from this area.

OREGON

This state hosts some of the truly fine steelhead streams of the Pacific Northwest. Unfortunately, many are not fished as heavily as they might be. Too many anglers feel they must head for famous streams like the Rogue or the North Umpqua and ignore other less famous—but possibly just as productive—streams.

Many streams in Oregon host excellent summer runs of steelhead. The Rogue is a classic example. The summer fish in the Rogue are small half-pounders for the most part but fun to catch and a thrill on a light flyrod.

License and tag fees for residents are as follows: Annual angling - $6.00; Daily angling - $2.50; Annual Juvenile angling - $2.00; Annual Salmon-Steelhead tag - $1.00. Nonresident annual angling - $20.00; 10-day angling - $10.00; Daily angling - $2.50; and Annual Salmon-Steelhead tag - $1.00.

Chetco River - The first steelhead river north of the California-Oregon border. The peak months for this winter stream are January and February. Fish average from eight pounds up. The river doesn't receive too much fishing pressure. Headquarters near Brookings on US 101.

Coos River - A pretty good river although it tends to discolor very readily under the smallest bit of rain. A small run of steelhead occurs during September and October but larger winter fish attract the attention of anglers during December and January. Located near Coos Bay on US 101.

Deschutes River - One of the mighty tributaries of the Columbia River. Known far and wide as a good producer of heavy steelhead. Located near Miller on Interstate 80N.

Nestucca River - A very popular river with Salem and Portland anglers. Good runs of steelhead usually arrive anytime after November 1. The runs normally peak during January or February. A good spot to fish is the tidal area near Pacific City. Located off US 101.

Nehalem River - A fairly short river but one very active with steelhead from January on through the spring. A good road parallels the stream from Nehalem upstream to Jewel. Located off highway US 101.

Rogue River - This is a river a writer could simply go overboard on. It has magic to it; small fish, big lunker steelhead, wild beautiful scenery, white water and so on. This is primarily a boating river and Rogue River drift boats are a common sight. The Rogue has a fine summer run of half-pound steelhead and the lower river is the best area. These fish have wide acclaim for their willingness to take wet flies. The best fishing for larger fish will be during September and October and from December through early spring. Fish the Gold Beach area off US 101 or Grants Pass-Medford area near US 99 on the upper river. The middle portion of the river is suitable for wading in many areas.

Siletz River - This river will generally have a good run of steelhead entering it anytime after November 1. Good roads are located nearby for anglers that wish to try new stretches of the river. The peak months are January and February. Located near Kernville off US 101.

Steelheading on Oregon's Deschutes River. *(Oregon Wildlife Commission photo)*

Sixes River - This river normally has very little fishing activity but it is a short and productive stream. Reaches its peak about December. Headquarter near the town of Sixes on US 101.

Smiths River - Another Oregon river with a small run of summer steelhead. This run peaks in June or July depending on the season. The winter run arrives with the winter rains and fish are usually available during November through January. An easily accessible river for fishermen. Located off US 201 near Reedsport.

Suislaw River - A good winter river with runs peaking during December and January. State Highway 36 provides access for fishermen to the bulk of the river's better drifts. Located near Florence off US 101.

Umpqua River - A large river with good wadable sections for anglers as well as heavy water better suited to drift boats. The North Fork of the Umpqua is acknowledged as one of the fine summer run streams devoted solely to flyfishing. The summer steelhead are large and the runs occur from June through August. Lower Umpqua water peaks out from November through February. The lower river is located off US 101 near Reedsport. The upper river is located near Roseburg off Interstate 5.

WASHINGTON

This state has over one hundred fifty streams that receive runs of steelhead. The rivers range in size from the huge Columbia River and its various tributaries to smaller more intimate streams shrouded in fog, mist and perpetual rain along the Olympic Peninsula. Many Washington streams are judged by the number of fish they produce annually as well as by the amount of access to the rivers by motorists. The rivers fished the hardest are those with highways running along their banks.

It must be remembered that much of Washington's steelhead range lies astraddle the Olympic Peninsula where daily rainstorms are a fact of life. Raingear is an essential part of the steelheader's clothing and high roily water is a daily hazard. But the steelhead fishing can be the finest in the country.

Additional information on steelhead fishing in Washington can be obtained from Washington Department of Natural Resources, General Administration Building, Olympia, WA 98501. Resident fishing and hunting licenses are $12.00; resident fishing - $7.50; county resident fishing - $6.00; 7-day non-resident fishing -$6.00; non-resident fishing - $20.00. Steelhead permit - $2.00.

Cowlitz River - This river is readily accessible to the vast hordes of fishermen living in the highly urbanized Seattle-Tacoma area. This is big water with good runs of winter steelhead. Best fishing occurs during the first three months of the year. Located near Kelso just off Interstate 5.

Duckabush River - This river receives a good run of summer steelhead during May and June. Winter steelhead arrive beginning in November and are present in fishable numbers through February. Located near Brinnon off US 101.

Green River - The Green flows right through the city of Seattle. Consequently it receives a great deal of fishing pressure. Runs peak during January and February. Good catches of steelhead are taken right in town and upstream in the upper reaches. The upper stretches are located off Interstate 90 near Palmer. Lower stretches can be reached via Interstate 5.

Hoh River - This river is a favorite of many Washington steelhead fishermen. It is a clear stream during cold weather months and produces good steelhead fishing. A road parallels the river giving access to fishermen. It features light fishing pressure when compared to other streams in the state. Best during the December through February period. It drains out of Olympic National Park and is reached via US 101 north of Queets. One of the best streams in Washington.

Humptulips River - A lightly-fished river on the Olympic Peninsula. Some very good steelhead are taken from this river during the December through February time. Located off US 101 near Humptulips.

Kalama River - A good late winter (March-April) river for nice steelhead. A combination boating-wading river. Located near Kelso off Interstate 5.

Puyallup River - Located near Tacoma off Interstate 5, this river is heavily fished near the cities. The upper Puyallup near Orting off Highway 162 can be very good at times. Top fishing occurs during February and March.

Queets River - Another Olympic Peninsula stream. This river could be one of the best rivers in the state if it received the angling pressure that is centered around the larger cities. A good winter (November-February) stream for nice fish. Bring raingear. Located off US 101 near Queets on the Pacific Ocean.

Quinault River - This river flows through the Quinault Indian Reservation and into the Pacific at Taholah. A good summer run during July. Winter fish ascend the stream from November through February. Indian guides are available at the reservation. Located off US 101 and State Highway 109.

Skagit River - The Skagit River is considered by many to be one of the classic steelhead streams along the Pacific Coast. A fine road parallels the river for miles. It receives its best winter run during February and March. Boating is the preferred way to fish the Skagit and guides are available at Sedro Woolley. Some bank fishing is done although it seems to be on a decline due to the intense boating activity. State Highway 20, from Interstate 5, will take you to Sedro Woolley and upstream toward the famous Sauk Pool.

Skykomish River - A very popular steelhead fly was named after this Washington river. A good river during December and January. The lower river is heavily fished but the upper reaches (near Gold Bar on US 2) have less pressure. The Skykomish River is reached via Interstate 5 near Everett. A famous stream in the Pacific Northwest.

Stillaguamish River - A good run of summer steelhead during July and August. The winter run occurs during January and February. The river is reached by traveling Interstate 5 north of Everett. One of the top streams in Washington.

Washougal River - Runs of winter steelhead arrive in this river in February and March and are of excellent size and quantity. Located near Vancouver off Highway 14.

IDAHO

The steelhead picture in Idaho is very sad. Catches of this majestic fish have been declining for several years. They experienced a real steelhead crisis in 1974 when a less than average run of fish in the Columbia River ran into difficulty before it reached Idaho waters.

Idaho fisheries people maintain they need at least 30,000 steelhead coming into Idaho to experience any type of fishing. The 1974 run totaled about 12,000 fish. The Fish and Game Commission closed the steelhead fishing entirely in October, 1974.

As this is being written, the Commission has also eliminated the spring steelhead season and the 1975 fall season is conditional upon the nature of the Columbia River run.

The best advice for anyone contemplating a trip to Idaho for steelhead would be to write for specific information. Contact the Idaho Fish and Game Department, P.O. Box 25, 600 S. Walnut St., Boise, ID 83707.

Clearwater River - This river system receives two runs of steelhead; one is a winter run which occurs usually during February-March-April and the fall run which begins in November and also continues through the winter months. This is primarily boat fishing below the dam at Lewiston off US 12. Big fish in this river system.

Salmon River - A river with very little access for steelheaders. Runs peak in this river at the same time as the Clearwater. Very difficult country to get into and out of just for a chance encounter with a steelhead.

BRITISH COLUMBIA

This expansive Canadian province has so many steelhead streams they are difficult to count or even to keep track of. The mainland and Vancouver Island teem with streams that receive runs of summer and winter steelhead.

Lists of summer steelhead streams are long indeed and many biologists and fishermen alike feel that only the surface has been scratched. When roads open up more of the wilderness, new streams will unfold to the watchful eye of prospecting steelheaders. Many of the rivers have never been charted, let alone fished.

The hard-to-get-at streams are scarcely fished—if at all. The easier streams to reach are being pounded pretty hard by both American and Canadian fishermen because of their relative ease of accessibility.

It should be pointed out that the use of roe as bait is banned on certain rivers. Some rivers also have a ban on fishing boats; these rivers must be fished either from shore or by wading.

British Columbia's Fish and Wildlife Branch, Parliament Buildings, Victoria, B.C. has a raft of fine bulletins outlining the steelhead fishery in their province. They can sum up the fishery in much better manner than I can in the limited space of this book.

License fees in British Columbia are: British Columbia resident (16-years and over) $5.00; resident of Canada (16 and over) $5.00, non-resident of Canada (16 years and older) $15.00; non-resident short term (three days) $6.00; B.C. resident steelhead license $3.00; Canadian resident (other than B.C.) steelhead license $10.00; non-resident steelhead license $10.00; special rivers license (non-resident) $25.00; and special lakes license (non-resident) $15.00.

Vancouver Island Streams

This island has a veritable horde of fine streams available for both winter and summer steelheading. The list is almost endless so to simplify matters immensely, allow me to merely name the streams and when they normally peak for steelhead. It would be impossible to give a thumbnail sketch of each. Detailed information on each stream could be obtained from the Fish and Wildlife Branch in Victoria or by contacting the Canadian Government Travel Bureau, Ottawa, Ontario, Canada.

Summer run steelhead are found in the following rivers: Nitinat, Klanawa, Sarita, China, Nahmint, Toquart, Moyeha, Heber, Stamp, Ash, and San Juan. Summer run steelhead are usually taken during July and August with the peak of the run occurring in these streams somewhere around August 1, depending on the seasons. Many of these summer streams receive very little, if any, fishing pressure. The potential of these streams has scarcely been tapped.

Many British Columbia natives, and some traveling steelhead fishermen from the States, feel that streams flowing from the west side of Vancouver Island are primarily summer steelhead streams. Those flowing from the east side of the Island are considered winter streams. There doesn't seem to be much basis in fact for this assumption, and sportsmen would be smart to overlook a good bit of this thinking and try for some winter fish on the west coast streams and summer fishing on some east coast streams. They might be pleasantly surprised.

Anyone with a yen for locating hot new fishing areas could have a field day in British Columbia with their summer run of steelhead. Countless streams harbor runs of hard fighting steelhead but very few have actually been fished.

Winter run steelhead are normally taken from Vancouver Island streams from the middle of December to the middle of

April. The peak of the spawning migration is from February 15
to March 15.

The better known and heaviest producing streams (again usu-
ally dependent upon access) are Cowichan, Nanaimo, Little
Qualicum, Puntledge, Oyster, Quinsam, Campbell, Salmon,
Nimpkish, Keogh, Kwatsi, San Juan, Stamp, Ash, Gold, Marble,
and Mhatta. Smaller streams that also provide good fishing are:
Chemainus, Englishman's, Big Qualicum, Tsable, Tsolum,
Sooke, and Jordon. Other lesser known winter steelhead
streams are Nitinat, Klahawa, Pachena, Sarita, Franklin, China,
Somass, Sproat, Nahmint, Toquart, Kennedy, Bedwell, Moyeha,
Burman and Heber.

Trying to put a steelheader's handle on the many and varied
steelhead streams along the mainland of British Columbia is
like pinning the tail on the donkey; it's almost impossible to do
with any degree of practicality. Roads are almost non-existent in
many of the better steelhead areas and virtually hundreds—
perhaps thousands—of small and large streams alike flow into
the Pacific Ocean along undisturbed beaches. Steelhead
streams are conspicuous by their sheer abundance but no one
seems to know for sure just which rivers are summer run or
which host winter fish, or a combination of the two. Cataloging
steelhead rivers along mainland British Columbia is a job that
apparently will take many years to complete—if it's ever possible.

The sheer problem of logistics is bound to confront B.C.
steelheaders. Other than a few well-known and heavily fished
areas, such as the Skeena River drainage system, many streams
either have no direct access to them or the problems of travel
are so difficult that the majority of fishermen would rather
dream of private streams where huge runs of gigantic steelhead
hold in quiet stretches at the bottom of a forgotten canyon, than
to try pursuing such a chancy dream. A steelheader just must
face the fact that these rivers are almost impossible to get at.

Many of the streams along the mainland are truly huge rivers
and to the angler not used to this factor, the transition from
small to big water can be both frightening and unproductive.

Highway 101 services just a very small portion of mainland
British Columbia. The road extends about 100 miles north of
Vancouver and deadends at the tiny village of Bliss Landing.
No other highway parallels the Strait of Georgia, Queen Char-
lotte Strait or the Pacific Ocean until the fisherman reaches

Prince Rupert, where Highway 16 curves in from the east. This is about 500 miles of roadless wilderness. In between lie countless steelhead rivers waiting for an inquisitive angler.

Highway 20 twists off from Highway 97 at Williams Lake and follows the Fraser River for a spell, saunters mightily along the Chilcotin and Chilanko rivers for a ways, and then parallels the Dean River before the road deadends at Bella Coola. The Fraser River is a huge river and very difficult for a wandering steelheader to fish. Chances of success on this river system lie in fishing some of the smaller sections of rivers such as the Thompson near Spences Bridge near the junction of Highways 8 and 97. The fishing here is usually at its best during December and January.

There are numerous rivers along Highway 101 from Vancouver north to Powell River and most of these hold winter and/or summer runs of steelhead. The best advice here would be for fishermen to seek advice from natives in the area. Streams such as Brem, Phillips, Theodosia, Vancouver, Brittain, Skwawka, Hunaschin Rivers and Wolfson Creek are some of the best bets in the Powell River area. Some of these rivers are accessible only by small boat and fishermen are hereby warned to be careful in many of the Inlets when using a small boat. The best fishing is normally from September through winter although January and February are probably the optimum period for fishing.

In the Sechelt area (Highway 101) there are some good steelhead streams available. I'd suggest trying Sechelt Creek, Chapman Creek, Rainy River, and McNair Creek. The best fishing in this area is normally late in the fall. Some accommodations are available for fishermen in this region.

The most renowned river system in the world for big steelhead is the Skeena River and its tributaries such as the Kispiox, Bulkley and Babine. This stretch of water reaches its peak anywhere from late August through October and these rivers represent the best opportunity for a fisherman to latch onto a twenty-pound steelhead and the outside chance of hooking into a thirty-pound plus fish.

The Kispiox is located near the town of New Hazelton on Highway 16. This river receives a good bit of runoff from headwaters and consequently is often high and dirty. Hit the Kispiox during low water and this has to be the premier steelhead stream in the world.

Early winter snow dots the riverbanks near Kamloops, British Columbia. *(Photo by the author)*

Steelhead taken from the Kispiox are normally sexually mature fish. They seem to ascend the river in a darkened color (males), and Kispiox steelhead tend to be heavier, thicker fish than others found in British Columbia waters.

The Kispiox is an easily wadable stream and steelhead hold in many of its lovely drifts. As long as the water level remains low and relatively clear, it is a fly fisherman's dream stream. High water conditions make it easier to fish with spinning or baitcasting gear.

The Babine River is also one of British Columbia's finest steelhead streams. It flows into the Skeena River some 50 miles above the town of Hazelton, which is just off Highway 16.

This river is little affected by rains because it runs out of Babine Lake. Steelhead fishing is normally at its peak during the month of October. Big fish of twenty pounds and more are available.

The Bulkley River is the largest branch of the Skeena River and enters the Skeena near Hazelton. It receives a good run of steelhead and normally peaks out sometime from November through January. Good for flyfishing during low clear water but more suitable for drift fishing during periods of high, discolored water.

There are a couple of other excellent steelhead streams in this immediate area such as the Morice near Houston, Sustut and Johanson Rivers near Terrace and the Kitsumkalum River north of Terrace. Normally excellent late fall and early winter fishing on these rivers.

ALASKA

All the problems of logistics are intensified for the Alaskan fisherman. Alaskan streams are almost all in remote areas far removed from civilization.

Solving the problems of how to get from point A to point B is the first major obstacle for steelheaders to overcome. The second hurdle would be to find someone, preferably a guide, to show you where and how to fish. Steelhead guides in Alaska are scarce. This means the problem of getting to the river and then knowing where to fish has been intensified. In a remote area where transportation is largely by air or boat, it also means that many of Alaska's streams are underfished, or not fished at all. Much of Alaska's fishing is done by natives that own an airplane or large boat and think nothing of charging off into the bush for a weekend of steelhead on some remote stream. Many of these streams will peak about September.

Alaska is still evaluating their steelhead streams and much of this information is still not complete. This much is known: Southeast Alaska (Region I) has over one thousand streams and about half of these support runs of steelhead. The best of these streams have an annual run of about three thousand fish, which is small compared to some of the runs in Washington, Oregon and British Columbia. It should be noted that all of Alaska's fish are wild native steelhead since the state does not have a steelhead hatchery program.

The bulk of Alaska's steelhead are found in the southeastern panhandle and northwestward to lower Cook Inlet and Kodiak Island. The bulk of the heaviest fishing occurs near population centers while many streams receive very little if any fishing pressure.

Many of Alaska's streams are small and steelhead are not too difficult to locate in low water. The average size fish will be close to eight or ten pounds in most rivers but some fish of twenty pounds or more have been taken.

Fishing licenses for residents cost $5.00 for annual sport fishing; resident hunting and sportfishing - $12.00; and resident hunting, trapping and sportfishing is $15. Non-resident sport fishing license - $20.00; visitor's special sportfishing license (10-day) - $10.00; and non-resident hunting and sportfishing license - $40.00. Other information on Alaska steelhead fishing can be obtained by writing State of Alaska Department of Fish and Game, Subport Building, Juneau, AK 99801.

Southeastern Area

Two separate runs of steelhead occur in the southeast area. In the lower southeast a fall run enters creeks that have an accessible lake in the system during September and peak in October. Excellent fishing is available through the winter. The Naha and Karta rivers near Ketchikan are the best choices. An excellent fall run enters the Situk River near Yakutat during October and November.

Spring runs enter the larger creeks in April and peak in May. Some of the better streams are Naha near Ketchikan; Klawak at Karta River; Eagle Creek on Prince of Wales; Snake Creek on Etolin; Sitkoh Creek on Chichagof; Pleasant Bay on Admiralty; Petersburg Creek near Petersburg and the Situk River at Yakutat.

Kenai Peninsula

Steelhead enters Anchor River, Deep Creek, Ninilchik River and Stariski Creek during August through October. September is the peak month. Some good flyfishing available on these streams.

Kodiak Islands

The Karluk River during October is one of the favorites among local anglers. Other suggested rivers would be the Fraser, Ayakulik (Red River) and Saltery.

Bristol Bay

Big silvery rainbows, often mistaken for steelhead, can be taken in the Kvichak (Lake Iliamna) and Naknek drainages. The best periods for fishing are during spring and fall.

Storied Steelhead
Streams East

W est Coast streams deserve credit for their role in elevating steelhead fishing to the fine sport it is today. But now many tributaries of the Great Lakes are becoming equally famous for their runs of big lake-run steelhead. Great Lakes steelhead streams, for the most part, are short and more placid rivers than those along the Pacific slope. Steelhead pause longer in deep pools and runs before pushing upstream toward the spawning grounds.

Many fishermen in this region are just beginning to learn about the fall-spawning steelhead available in many rivers. These fish add a bright new dimension to fall fishing as bright silver-clad females and broad-shouldered, thick bucks ascend the rivers in later October and November for actual fall spawning.

Storied steelhead streams of the Great Lakes region are equally rich in steelhead as their West Coast cousins, although the legends that make a stream world-famous are newer and fresher.

It is unfortunate, however, that at this time the states of New York and Pennsylvania do not have their steelhead programs geared up to match those of Michigan, Wisconsin, Minnesota and Ontario. The southern Great Lakes states of Ohio, Indiana and Illinois are producing good catches of steelhead although on a somewhat limited basis and in very restricted areas. The three Upper Great Lakes states and Ontario now offer the fisherman his best shot at fishing a Midwest storied stream.

At the top of the list of all-time favorites is Michigan's Little Manistee River. This river is host to huge spring runs of steelhead that average ten pounds, a goodly number of fifteen to twenty-pound fish being taken every spring. A large percentage of the steelhead planted in the Great Lakes tributaries are fish raised from fertilized eggs taken from fish at the Little Manistee weir.

The run begins with fall fish, mostly bucks, migrating upstream during November and December and wintering in the river. The hens make their spawning run during March or April, depending on the weather conditions.

Thousands of fishermen invade the Little Manistee every spring when the early steelhead season opens in April. The reliability of the stream is governed to a large degree by rainfall. Heavy rains put the river over its banks and it is almost unfishable. But, to many anglers, the chances of getting a crack at a twenty-pound steelhead is enough to warrant waiting out high water and muddy conditions.

The nearby Big Manistee River is another storied stream. Unlike the Little Manistee's unimpeded stream flow, the Big Manistee is dominated by huge Tippy Dam that controls the flow of current and halts any further upstream steelhead migration.

The Big River, as some of the natives call it, receives a very large run of steelhead that rank among the largest found in the United States. This is a large deep heavy-currented river that is best fished by boat or from the bank. Very few locations lend themselves to wading. Fish over twenty pounds are taken every year although the numbers of these larger steelhead are few indeed. The average sized fish would be around ten to twelve pounds.

The crystal-clear Platte River in Michigan is another of the storied steelhead streams of the Great Lakes region. This river is so shallow in places that steelhead must shoulder upstream over gravel bars with parts of their backs splitting the surface of the river. Steelhead in the Platte average close to ten pounds with occasional fish nudging the twenty-pound mark. This short stream pours its waters into Lake Michigan. A superb river-mouth hosts hundreds of steelhead during fall months and provides an excellent openwater fishery for anglers. One of the Great Lakes best fall spawning steelhead streams.

Just as the Rogue River was made famous by Zane Grey, the Big Two Hearted River was immortalized by Ernest Hemingway in his stories of Michigan's Upper Peninsula.

The Big Two Hearted is a fine spring and fall stream. The fish aren't as large as those entering more southerly streams but the competition isn't as keen, the river is a tannic acid color flowing through a beautiful river valley, and the fish—fresh in from Lake Superior—are sleek and sassy and full of fight. Ernest Hemingway knew a classic steelhead stream when he saw one.

The Bois Brule in northern Wisconsin is considered by many Midwestern steelhead fishermen to be one of the most reliable steelhead rivers in the Great Lakes area. This river is called the Brule by many of the locals, but it is not to be confused with a mediocre stream of the same name in Minnesota. The Bois Brule flows north into Lake Superior and receives a very dependable run of steelhead in spring and late fall. Many anglers consider this stream to be one of the finest in the Midwest although I personally do not think it rates quite as highly as some of the Michigan streams.

Several rivers flowing into the northern shore of Lake Superior rank as Minnesota's contribution to Great Lakes steelhead fishing. I personally rank the Reservation River as being one of the topnotch steelhead streams in Minnesota. The fish do not run nearly as large as in other streams but the cold water of Lake Superior, and the fish's fatfree diet, makes them a test of any angler's skill. Productive fishing in the Reservation is limited primarily to May and early June, but there are normally good numbers of fish available during that time.

Ontario, with her huge sprawling shoreline along Lakes Superior and Huron, offers the steelhead fisherman a couple of classic trout streams that produce excellent steelhead fishing.

The Michipicoten River near Wawa is one of Ontario's most productive streams although this sparsely settled northern shore of Lake Superior hosts some of the finest and yet secluded steelhead fishing in North America.

The Michipicoten River is a fairly large river best fished by a

combination of boat and wading. A small boat can take the angler to narrow stretches of river where he can fish gravel-studded
runs where fresh run steelhead hold before pushing upstream to
the spawning grounds. The only company most fishermen
might find along this river would be an occasional shuffling
black bear or a bald eagle perched in the top of a weather-
beaten spruce. This river is a swift boulder-strewn stream that
makes for extremely difficult wading but the seclusion and fast
fishing often outweighs any problems involved in fishing.

Another classic steelhead stream in Ontario is the Nottawasaga River in the Georgian Bay area of Lake Huron.
Steelhead ascending this river rank among some of the largest
taken in Ontario waters and every year husky fifteen to
twenty-pound specimens are taken by skillful anglers.

Storied steelhead streams are one notch above the ordinary;
the angler expects something special from these Great Lakes
rivers and he normally receives it. These rivers have built a last-
ing reputation by their sheer beauty, productivity, and continuing good fishing for a great number of fishermen.

GREAT LAKES STREAMS

Great Lakes steelhead streams take many forms, ranging from
short placid streams with a meager population of steelhead to
the more noteworthy rivers of large, heavy flow and tremendous
annual migrations of silvery steelhead from the big lakes.

It should be pointed out that some truly excellent offshore
fishing exists adjacent to the mouths of the steelhead streams
listed below. Many anglers are overlooking some great fishing
at the rivermouths. Steelhead have to pass through the rivermouths to enter the streams and these are concentration points
that bear further investigation.

MICHIGAN

The Wolverine State is undoubtedly the hottest state in the
Great Lakes for steelhead fishing. A variety of fishing opportunities presents itself to fishermen. A fisherman with a bit of
knowledge can find topnotch steelhead fishing during almost
any season of the year. This is the only Midwestern state offering steelhead during all seasons of the year. Steelhead are taken
by trollers on the Great Lakes during all periods of open water.

Steelhead are in various rivers from September through May and at least one stream has summer steelhead during July and August.

The daily possession limit is a generous five fish, and when you consider the average Michigan steelhead is around ten pounds, that amounts to a hefty catch of fish. A resident fishing license and trout stamp is $6.50; non-resident season fishing license and trout stamp goes for $9.50; a 7-day non-resident license good for all species is $5.25; a 3-day good for all species is $2.25 and a 1-day Great Lakes only license is $1.25.

Further information on Michigan fishing for steelhead can be obtained from Michigan Department of Natural Resources, Fisheries Division, Stevens T. Mason Building, Lansing, MI 48926; Michigan Travel Commission, 300 S. Capitol Ave., Lansing, MI 48993; or Upper Peninsula Travel and Recreation Association, P.O. Box 400, Iron Mountain, MI 49801.

Lake Michigan Streams:

Betsie River - located near Beulah along US 31. A steady producer of big steelhead in the ten to eighteen-pound class during March and April and again during October through December. A dirty-colored stream at all times. Very difficult wading and too small for a boat. One of Michigan's top steelhead streams. The "odd" summer steelhead is taken during July and August.

Black River - a sleeper steelhead stream in southern Michigan near South Haven. Steelhead range up to fifteen pounds although a six to eight-pound fish is closer to the average. Best fishing is February through April during the spring spawn. Easily accessible off US 31.

Boardman River - located in Traverse City and crossed by US 31, this river has a good run of steelhead in sizes from two pounds up to ten pounds. Smaller fish are more common. The bulk of the fishing is done off the rivermouth during April and May. Primarily a boat fishery off the rivermouth although some bank fishing can be done in places.

Elk River - a very short (one-half mile) river flowing into Lake Michigan at the town of Elk Rapids along US 31. In the clear part of the river below the power dam, the steelhead are easily spotted by anglers, and as a consequence this area gets fished extremely hard. Best fishing is in April and early May. Try the rivermouth for occasional excellent fishing.

One of the storied steelhead streams of Michigan. *(Michigan Tourist Council photo)*

Grand River - The best fishing is below the Grand River dam in Grand Rapids. Deep, treacherous water and best fished from shore. March-April and October through December. Some big steelhead.

Little Manistee - Possibly the finest steelhead stream in the country - at least in Michigan. Huge runs of big ten to twenty-pound steelhead during April and again during October through December. Best fishing occurs in the Stronach area upstream to Irons (several miles east of US 31 near Manistee). Some excellent steelhead are taken at the mouth of the Little Manistee where it empties into Manistee Lake at Manistee. A river easily roiled by rain or runoff but highly productive. Probably the heaviest-fished steelhead river in the Midwest. Avoid the weekends.

Manistee River - The Big Manistee, downstream from Tippy Dam (just off highways M55 and US 31), is one of Michigan's finest streams. A big, dangerous river, it is best suited to boat fishing although wading is possible for a short distance downstream from the dam. Big fish fall regularly to hardware and lure fishermen, while bait fishermen take primarily smaller fish. Scarcely affected by high waters, rain or snow. Fish bite best on rising water.

Muskegon River - Another topnotch steelhead stream governed by massive Croton Dam upstream about fifty miles from the rivermouth at Muskegon. Good fishing is available throughout the river system downstream from Croton (near Newaygo and about thirty miles east of US 31) although some of the best fishing is from Croton to Newaygo. February through April and again during October through December. More water available for the wader although canoe and boat fishermen can cover the drifts. A big fish river.

Platte River - A gin-clear stream with a large run of spring and fall spawning steelhead. April and November through December are the top months. A superb rivermouth for steelhead fishing during October. Fish average close to 10 pounds with many fish much larger. A narrow stream with plenty of obstacles for the fisherman to contend with. An excellent steelhead producer but very heavily fished.

St. Joseph River - a new and fantastic steelhead fishery has erupted on this river near the town of Berrien Springs in the southwest corner of the state. Fish up to twenty pounds are taken below the Berrien Springs dam. Flatfish and Tadpollies are the best lures; spawn bags take some of the smaller fish. Winter fishing is first class on this river for those willing to brave the ten-degree winter breezes and swirling snow storms. A hot new Michigan river soon to develop a nation-wide reputation.

Lake Huron Streams:

AuSable River - this large river is controlled by Foote Dam west of Oscoda and just off US 23. A fair winter stream, fishing takes off with excellent catches of eight to twelve-pound steelhead during March, April, and May. One of the few rivers in lower Michigan with a good spring run extending into May. Hot action again during November-December. A good river for drift boats or small cartoppers.

East Branch AuGres River (Whitney Drain) - a surprisingly good producer during March and April and again during October-December. A shallow wadable river with a good run of six to twelve-pound fish. Definitely an underfished stream. Located near highways M55 and US 23. Plan on fishing the rivermouth in the fall.

Ocqueoc River - A sleeper stream with good runs of fish up to fifteen pounds although the average is a good bit smaller with six to eight pound fish much more common. Deep holes just up from the rivermouth are some of the best fishing spots in the river. April and early May are best times for fishing.

Rifle River - This is a newly-stocked steelhead stream that shows a promise of becoming one of the top Lake Huron rivers. Too early to tell at this writing how this river will produce but it bears watching. Located off US 23 near Omer and AuGres.

Sturgeon River - This is a favorite of mine. Located in the middle of the Lower Peninsula of Michigan, it receives a run of fish from Burt Lake near the town of Indian River just off old US 27. It features good runs of smallish (three to eight-pound) fish during April and early May, and again during October through December. This river also features a summer run of steelhead (two to four pounds) during July and August. The lower end of the river is best for summer fish while spring and fall steelhead spread throughout the river from Wolverine to Indian River.

Lake Superior Streams:

Chocolay River - a tannic acid-stained river near Marquette (off M41) that produces good runs of steelhead during late April and early May. A smaller run occurs during November. Tough wading for anglers unaccustomed to wading dark water. Seldom fished.

Middle Branch Ontonagon River - Steelhead are blocked from further upstream migration on this river by towering and beautiful Agate Falls. Superb April and May fishing for steelhead up to ten pounds. Smaller fish are more plentiful. A spectacular river to fish. Easily wadable. Located on highway M28 near Bruce Crossing.

Mosquito River - A very difficult river for anglers to reach, but not for big Lake Superior steelhead. This river is located northeast of Munising near the tiny village of Melstrand. Dirt trails lead to the river and are often impassable during spring snow melts and rainstorms. Good fishing at the rivermouth as well as in the log-infested river itself. Big fish are common (many over ten pounds) but often break off in the debris-filled water.

Two Hearted River - A gentle tea-colored stream with a good run of steelhead during late April and throughout May. Some fishing during October and November. Located almost straight north of Newberry; this river is also rather difficult to reach although dirt roads traverse the sandy pine country immortalized by Ernest Hemingway years ago. Accommodations are limited at the mouth of the river and many fishermen bring their own truck campers or vans and camp in various parks. A good rivermouth for surf fishing or trolling.

WISCONSIN

This state features some very good steelhead fishing although it has very few steelhead runs comparable to Michigan's. A great deal of Wisconsin's steelhead fishing revolves around open water fishing in Lake Michigan and to a smaller degree, Lake Superior.

Most of the streams flowing into Lake Michigan are short and rather sluggish and many steelhead attempt spawning in open water shoal areas where natural reproduction is destined to failure. Annual stockings maintain their excellent fishing. Most of

the rivers support anadromous runs only when water temperatures permit.

Lake fishing for steelhead takes place year around in Wisconsin with spring, summer and fall anglers catching fish by trolling, bait fishing or casting lures from shore, off piers jutting
into the lake, or by wading and casting.

Casting small spoons and spinners from the limestone shelfs
around Door County (Highways 42 and 57) is extremely productive during March and April.

Wisconsin anglers fishing Lake Michigan caught more
steelhead during the 1974 fishing season than any previous
year.

Fishing license for non-resident annual is $12.50; family
fishing—$18.00; 15-day - $7.50; and 4-day - $5.50. Additional
information can be obtained by writing to Department of Natural Resources, Fisheries Division, P.O. Box 450, Madison, WI.

Lake Michigan Streams:

Riebolts Creek - This tiny stream is located at the head of
Moonlight Bay just north of the town of Bailey's Harbor and just
off Highway 57. It receives excellent runs of steelhead whenever water conditions permit. Much of the river is state owned
and easily accessible. Best fishing normally during April.
Sporadic runs demand excellent timing.

Heins Creek - This small stream is the outlet of Kangaroo
Lake and is located just south of Bailey's Harbor and crosses
Highway 57. It has about a mile of excellent fishing water and
holds many steelhead in its brushy holes during April. Heavily
fished when the steelhead are running.

Hibbards Creek - One of Wisconsin's best Lake Michigan
tributaries with almost two miles of fine steelhead water. It is
best during April and is located near the town of Jacksonport on
Highway 57.

Whitefish Bay Creek - This short stream is the outlet of Clarks
Lake and is a very clear stream, which makes for extremely difficult but challenging steelhead fishing. This river is about
halfway between Sturgeon Bay and Jacksonport.

Ahnapee River - This is one of the major steelhead streams in
Wisconsin with good fishing during April. Good fish are found
right up to the dam at Forestville (Highway 42).

Kewaunee River - This is a very big river and probably the best bet for steelheaders. Large numbers of fish use the river and it has over ten miles of good holding water. Some of the tributaries also hold fish during April. Can be waded in places or fished by boat. Located at the town of Kewaunee.

Manitowoc River - This is also a very big river with concentrations of steelhead building up beneath the dam at Manitowoc Rapids. Best fishing is during April.

Lake Superior Streams:

Cranberry River - This is a small stream near Ashland but is considered by many steelheaders to be one of the best rivers in the area. Fourteen miles of heavy brush cover makes this a very challenging river to fish. Steelhead average about four to eight pounds and provide a worthy scrap in the tight quarters. Best fishing occurs during April and May.

Fish Creek - This small river has some 10 miles of excellent water comprised of both farmland fishing and wild country angling. Fishing is best with light line for the smaller steelhead during April.

Bois Brule River - This is the most famous and well-known steelhead stream in northern Wisconsin. A special season for anadromous fish limits the open fishing water to twenty miles of the river. Check for up-to-date regulations. This river is full of holes, runs, and shallow gravel bars where migrating steelhead can pause to rest or spawn. Located near the town of Brule along US 2. Big fish are fairly common with a steelhead of ten to twelve pounds being tops although smaller four to six pounders are more prevalent.

MINNESOTA

Steelhead fishing in Minnesota will be getting a new lease on life with the building of the new French River salmon hatchery in 1975. Steelhead raised in this hatchery will be planted in rivers flowing into the North Shore of Lake Superior.

To further help steelhead toward natural reproduction, the Minnesota DNR, funded by the Anadromous Fish Act of Congress, is removing upstream barriers along some North Shore streams that have inhibited steelhead movements for countless years. Barrier alteration has been completed on the Lester, Knife and Sucker Rivers, and barrier removal is being planned

The north shore of Lake Superior in Minnesota is considered by many Great Lakes steelheaders to be a hotspot. *(State of Minnesota photo)*

for the Stewart River. All told over 75 miles of stream along the North Shore has been enhanced under this project.

Steelhead ascend most of the streams from Duluth north.

Fishing licenses in Minnesota cost $4.00 for the resident husband and $6.00 for husband and wife. Non-resident fishing license fees are $6.50 for individual, $10.00 for combination husband and wife, and $3.00 for a three-day license.

North Shore streams have been noted for their steelhead fishing for many years, and steelhead now account for more than ninety percent of the stream trout taken below the barrier falls. There are fifty-nine streams along the North Shore which attract steelhead spawning runs and they provide about one hundred thirty-two miles of accessible water to these fish. The amount of fishable water available to steelhead and steelhead fishermen ranges from as little as sixty-five feet in Onion Creek to as much as seventy miles in the Knife River.

Minnesota considers her steelhead fishing as a "trophy fishery". A recent yearly census on North Shore streams showed 20,000 to 22,000 anglers fishing for a total catch of some five thousand to eight thousand steelhead over a 50,000-hour span of man hours on the streams. But, the chances of latching onto a 12-pound steelhead in one of the picturesque gorges of the North Shore makes the prospects a very heady experience. Write the Minnesota Department of Natural Resources, Section of Fisheries, Division of Fish and Wildlife, Centennial Office Building, St. Paul, MN 55155 for more information.

Lake Superior Streams:

Baptism River - This river has less than a mile of accessible water open to steelhead fishing. Best fishing normally occurs during May. This river is located about fifty miles up the shoreline from Duluth.

Brule (Arrowhead) River - Another short river with only about one and a half miles of stream open for steelhead fishing. Best time of the year is during May. This river is about twenty miles from Grand Marais.

Knife River - Minnesota's longest steelhead river system. This stream has over seventy miles of accessible fishing area and the fishing can be very good at times. Off shore fishing is excellent at the mouth of the Knife. River fishing is best during May while open water fishing hits its stride during June through August. The Knife is located just a few miles outside Duluth and consequently bears a large amount of fishing pressure.

Sucker River - Located near Duluth and Two Harbors, the Sucker has another extremely short stretch of fishable water— only .38 mile—and the best fishing seems to be near the rivermouth and also out in the open water of the lake. May is the best month for river fishing while the open water fishery holds up well through September.

ONTARIO

This Canadian province has a widely diversified steelhead fishery. Fishing possibilities range from quaint streams flowing through meadows to rushing torrents of whitewater cascading into Lake Superior. Some of the Lake Superior streams are so remote that only a prospecting fisherman, by boat, could sample them all, and that might take him several years.

Some Ontario streams, because of their very remoteness, are seldom, if ever fished. The North Shore of Lake Superior is a classic example; many streams are fairly short and are not crossed by any highway. Consequently, the only way to get to them is to bust through the bush country or launch a seaworthy boat at the closest launching site and motor into the area, stopping at every rivermouth to sample the fishing. If you test enough areas at the proper time of year, you're sure to hit a silvery jackpot.

Steelhead runs are often a very difficult thing to hit at the right time along the Lake Superior shoreline. Many times the spring run lasts only a week or so, and the angler must be there at exactly the right time. It pays to make some type of contact either with a local outfitter, guide, or possibly a local chamber of commerce, if they will reveal the name of a further reliable contact.

Lake Superior streams are normally underfished except on those rivers where the road lays nearby or where the stream is crossed by a major highway. Even these streams, a half-mile or mile away, are seldom sampled by steelheaders. It often pays to go exploring on these tributaries although the angler should always make adequate preparations. Much of this land is roadless wilderness and many fishermen have become turned around

The Nottawasaga River in Ontario is a fly fisherman's dream. *(Ontario Ministry of Industry and Tourism photo)*

while trying to take a shortcut back to their car or camp. Carry a compass in the Canadian bush and know how to use it.

Streams flowing into Lake Huron and adjacent Georgian Bay are well known to Great Lakes steelhead fishermen and very often these rivers are filled to fisherman capacity during the spring runs.

Steelhead from the Lake Huron area tend to weigh a great deal more than their Lake Superior kin. This is due, in part, to the rich diet of alewives and smelt found in offshore waters.

There are some small inconsequential steelhead runs in several tributaries along both Lake Erie and Lake Ontario. At this time these runs contribute very little to the overall catch ratio of steelhead in Ontario.

Ontario residents do not require a fishing license to participate in their sport in Ontario waters. Other Canadian residents are required to purchase a Canadian resident angling license for $4.00; a non-resident Canadian organized camp angling license is $10.00; a non-resident season angling license is $10.75; non-resident 3-day license is $6.00; and non-resident organized camp angling license is $10.00.

Steelhead fishermen desiring additional information concerning Ontario fishing should contact Ministry of Industry and Tourism, Hearst Block, Queen's Park, Toronto, Ontario M7A 1T2 or Canadian Government Travel Bureau, Office of Tourism, Ottawa, Ontario K1A OH6.

Lake Superior Streams:

Agawa River - A swift-flowing stream that receives an excellent run of five to 10-pound steelhead during the spring run in May. Occasionally runs occur as late as June, depending on the weather. The river is located off Queen's Highway 17 approximately halfway between Sault Ste. Marie and Wawa, Ontario. A wadable river.

Baldhead River - Another fine steelhead stream but one largely removed from any highway. Best reached by boat from Wawa or the Montreal River harbor. It is located in Lake Superior Provincial Park about thirty to forty miles southeast of Wawa. Steelhead range up to 10 pounds although smaller ones are much more common. An excellent secluded and seldom-fished river.

Coldwater River - This fine stream is located near the Baldhead but is located much closer to Highway 17. Steelhead are fairly small although prospecting fishermen near the rivermouth often pick up nice-sized fish. Can be reached via the highway or by boat. Rivermouth prospecting by boat can be a very productive method of fishing. Can be easily waded.

Michipicoten River - This is one of Ontario's more productive steelhead streams. Guide service is located in nearby Wawa and much of the fishing is done from riverboats or by wading. Steelhead range up to 10 or 12 pounds although five and six-pounders are more common. Large concentrations of steelhead in May and again during the fall runs in October and November.

Montreal River - Steelhead are taken in large numbers below the Montreal River Gorge, which lays astraddle Highway 17. This is an excellent steelhead river although it does not lend itself to wading. Primarily boat or shore fishing. Wading is practical near the rivermouth. Some big steelhead are taken from this river. May is the best time.

Old Woman River - This cheery little river is a good bet for wading anglers. It is easily fished and steelhead lay in predictable locations. The river lays just a few miles from Wawa and crosses Highway 17. Move away from the road toward the Lake Superior shoreline for best action. Best during May.

University River - Another excellent bet for May steelhead. A wadable river that produces steelhead up to 10 pounds. It is located just west of Wawa off Highway 17.

There are countless other small and lesser known steelhead rivers flowing into the North Shore of Lake Superior. Excellent runs have been reported in many of the smaller rivers lying between Wawa and Marathon but most of this is roadless bush country where only the angler intent on locating untapped fishing hotspots ventures. A boat is very handy for fishing the rivermouths and for traveling from one river to another. A word of caution: *keep an eye on the weather over Lake Superior.* Storms build up quickly. Check with the Ontario Provincial Police or the Royal Canadian Mounted Police and leave word on where you are going and when you plan to return.

Lake Huron and Georgian Bay Streams:

Bighead River - This river is located near the town of Meaford on Highway 26 and flows into Lake Huron's Georgian Bay.

Steelhead runs normally occur during April and occasionally into May. Some big fish up to fifteen pounds although the average is about half that.

BlueJay Creek - A small stream located on Manitoulin Island in northern Lake Huron. Some nice steelhead are taken from this small stream during April and May. A novel area to fish steelhead.

Nottawasaga River - One of Lake Huron's most highly respected steelhead rivers. Big fish come into this river during April and again during the October-November periods. An easily wadable stream. Located near Barrie off Highway 26. This river flows into Nottawasaga Bay at the lower end of Georgian Bay.

Manitou River - Another fine steelhead stream located on Manitoulin Island. Some big fish although the average steelhead would be around five or six pounds. April fishing.

Saugeen River - This highly productive stream flows into Lake Huron at Southampton on Highway 21. The Saugeen has the enviable reputation for producing some of the biggest Ontario steelhead. It is a heavily fished stream that is easily wadable. A good bet for fishermen. Best fishing during April and May and again during November.

Lake Erie Streams:

Steelhead runs in Ontario waters of Lake Erie are not very productive although some nice fish do occasionally show up. The small numbers of fish available make proper timing essential.

I'd suggest trying Big Otter, Venison, Clear, Dedrich and Young Creeks for a shot at Lake Erie steelhead. A local contact or visit to the Ministry of Natural Resources offices in Toronto should give you more information.

Lake Ontario Streams:

Streams entering Lake Ontario also have very small and highly localized steelhead runs. I'd suggest trying Wilmot Stream, Ganaraska Stream, Shelter Valley Stream, Bowmanville Creek and Soper Creek. These streams currently providing a limited brand of steelhead fishing.

OHIO

Steelhead have been stocked into northeastern Ohio streams, that are part of the Lake Erie drainage, since 1969. At the present time there is a very limited steelhead fishery available in Ohio. Only two streams are stocked every spring with trout fingerlings obtained from federal fish hatcheries. Ohio is currently planting a wild strain of Michigan steelhead and plans are to restock some of the same streams again in future years.

The best fishing occurs from mid-fall to mid-spring. A creel census of Ohio's steelhead waters shows some steelhead taken in the eight to eleven-pound class although most of the fish fall into the three to four-pound class.

License fees and where to write for information: Ohio resident license fees are $4.50; annual non-resident - $10.50; 7-day non-resident - $4.50. For additional information contact Ohio Department of Natural Resources, Division of Wildlife, Fountain Square, Columbus OH 43224.

Lake Erie Streams:

Chagrin River - The best fishing is to be found near the towns of Eastlake and Willoughby. Daniels Park, near Willoughby, is another favorite location on this river. These towns are located just east of Cleveland. The Chagrin is a wadable river and the best months to fish are in March and April and again during October and November.

Conneaut Creek - Most of the steelhead fishing on Conneaut Creek occurs in the vicinity of Conneaut, in the extreme northeastern corner of Ohio. A wadable stream, some nice steelhead are taken from its waters. Best during March-April and October-November.

Some steelhead fishing is available in the Lake Erie tributaries of Arcola and Turkey creeks and the Rocky River. These areas have limited access.

PENNSYLVANIA

The bulk of Pennsylvania's steelhead fishing lies along a stretch of Erie County called "Rainbow Run". This is a collective name for the Erie County streams emptying into Lake Erie. These creeks attract anglers from across the nation during spring and fall when big steelhead migrate upstream.

Open water fishing for steelhead is normally good off river-mouths during October as the streams attract spawning hordes of coho and chinook salmon.

License fees are for resident - $7.50; non-resident - $12.50; 7-day tourist license - $7.50; and $2.00 for a senior resident. A $.25 issuing agent's fee is charged on all licenses.

Additional information can be obtained by writing Pennsylvania Fish Commission, P.O. Box 1678, Harrisburg, PA 17120 or Greater Erie Chamber of Commerce, Erie, PA 16501.

Lake Erie Streams:

Elk Creek - A small stream that receives a big run of steelhead from Lake Erie. It is located near Lake City off Highway 90. A wadable stream that produces big steelhead up to fifteen pounds. Six to eight pounders are more common. Best fishing is from mid-April through May and again during October off the rivermouth.

Twenty Mile Creek - Another small river that is easily wadable and it too receives good runs of steelhead in April and May. Located in the eastern corner of Erie County just off Highway 90. Good rivermouth fishing during fall months. Some fish up to thirty-three inches.

Walnut Creek - Another small stream that receives one of Pennsylvania's largest steelhead runs during spring months. It is located just west of the city of Erie off Highways 5 and 20. Good rivermouth fishing in October.

Other top Pennsylvania streams for steelhead are Trout Run, Crooked Creek, Raccoon Creek, Elk Creek, Six Mile Creek, Seven Mile Creek, Eight Mile Creek, Twelve Mile Creek, Sixteen Mile Creek and scattered locations along the Lake Erie shoreline.

NEW YORK

New York has a limited steelhead fishery along certain areas of both Lake Ontario and Lake Erie. This fishery is concentrated primarily offshore of various towns along the shorelines.

Fishing hinges on weather, temperature of the water and the number and ages of returning steelhead.

Lake Ontario fishing areas

The bulk of New York's steelhead fishing centers around the cities of Pulaski, Altmar and Orwell. The Salmon River near Pulaski has a small run of steelhead returning during the spring and fall months for spawning. This is not a reliable run although, under perfect situations, a fisherman can find excellent angling.

Lake Erie fishing areas

Fishing the open water areas of Lake Erie near the cities of Dunkirk, Barcelona, Hamburg and Buffalo produces some steelhead for New York Anglers. Silver Creek, near the city of the same name off Interstate 90, is probably the best bet for river fishing for steelies. A small wadable stream that hosts a small run of fish from Lake Erie. Proper timing is extremely important.

INDIANA

This state has the smallest amount of land bordering any of the Great Lakes but don't let its shoreline size fool you. Indiana yearly produces some of the lunker steelhead taken from Lake Michigan waters.

The state doesn't have too much to offer in the line of streams to attract steelhead, although there are two rivers that host a small run of fish. There is a pretty firm indication that the Little Calumet River near Gary is hosting a small run of summer steelhead up to six pounds. If so, this will be electrifying news to steelhead fishermen in the Midwest.

Most of the steelhead fishing takes place in Lake Michigan waters as anglers troll for other species. Michigan City is one of the hotspots for trolling during spring (just after ice-out) and throughout the summer. Gary, Indiana fishermen take a healthy number of steelhead for about two or three months after ice-out.

A resident fishing license and trout stamp costs $5.75; non-resident angling and trout stamp is $7.00; and a 14-day fishing license costs $3.25. For additional information on steelhead fishing in Indiana write: Indiana Department of Natural Resources, Fisheries Division, 607 State Office Building, Indianapolis, IN 46204.

Lake Michigan Streams:

Little Calumet River - This river located near Gary does not look like a steelhead stream but it hosts small runs of some very big fish. Indiana's state record steelhead is over 20 pounds and fishermen hang big fish from the Little Calumet River every year. It is best during March and April and again during the fall months of October and November.

Trail Creek - A small stream that receives a small run of steelhead during the spring and fall months. Not "trouty" looking at all but it does support a run of some very large steelhead. Located near Trail Creek and Michigan City.

ILLINOIS

Another state possessing a very small portion of Lake Michigan real estate. The bulk of the steelhead taken here are by trollers plying offshore waters for other species.

All plantings of steelhead are made directly into Lake Michigan and the Illinois Division of Fisheries are planning plants of some 100,000 fish yearly.

The ports of Waukegan, Diversey and Jackson receive the yearly plants and this is the area where the majority of Illinois steelhead are taken.

License fees for residents are $2.25; non-resident is $4.25 and a 10-day non-resident license costs $2.25. Additional information on Illinois fishing can be obtained by writing Illinois Department of Conservation, Division of Fisheries, 605 State Office Building, 400 S. Spring Street, Springfield, IL 62706.

Unstoried Steelhead Streams

All the West Coast and Great Lakes states have any number of undiscovered small tributaries or larger rivers. Many streams are misleadingly listed as not containing "significant" populations of trout. Most states, my home state of Michigan, for instance, are on the clean water bandwagon, which is heartening to see. And, as these rivers are cleaned up, silt and pollution removed, the rivers have the chance to cleanse themselves and become more attractive to steelhead. Many formerly polluted streams which in years past hosted only large concentrations of carp or other rough fish now receive runs of steelhead.

And, if the truth were known, all too many anglers seek out the big-name streams because everyone knows where to go on the river for the best action. If the run is on in that river, and you happen to get into a hotspot right away, you come away from the trip with a smug feeling.

But if the day turns sour, fishermen are more plentiful than fish, and you feel like you should have stayed home—or gone exploring—then perhaps that's just what you should have done.

Unexploited steelhead streams are like pearls in oysters: some streams have fish and some don't. The only way to find out which is which is to fish them. Try enough streams in enough areas and you'll soon learn which are productive and which you should bypass in the future.

Many states adopt the philosophy of closing certain sections of a steelhead stream to protect the spawning fish. These areas normally open up after the bulk of the steelhead have spawned. There are times when the weatherman doesn't cooperate with the fish and spring arrives late. When this happens, excellent fishing can often be found in the headwaters of these streams, if headwater fishing is legal in your area, during late winter or the spring.

Many fishermen maintain friendships with the local fish warden or conservation officer. These men are dedicated to the fish they protect, but it is also part of their job to divulge fishing information if it isn't injurious to the fishery. Many officers know of runs in certain streams that aren't being fished, and it often takes only a few minutes of your time to learn about some fantastic fishing.

Many steelhead hotspots on unknown streams will be found by sheer determination. This means traveling long dusty miles down dirt trails and searching old maps and logging trails for signs of streams.

A trick some steelheaders use is to win the confidence of state surveyors or department of transportation officials. The next step is to secure maps at least 20 years old that show old logging roads. Many of these roads will be almost overgrown today, but trails will remain. Newer maps usually omit these older trails. Some surveyors and state men do this on purpose; some have been known to purposely omit known beaverponds, etc. You may be surprised at what an old set of maps may show you.

As I sit typing this chapter a large river north of me is experiencing its first steelhead run. The plantings of steelhead were duly recorded by fisheries people and the local newspapers; but those fish were planted two or three years ago—and people forget. How many fishermen were present today when I checked the river? Not a one. The steelhead could be seen scooting up the fish ladder, fish were seen in shallow water on the redds, but the fishermen had stayed home. Steelhead plants should be either mentally or physically noted and a follow-up check should be made in two or three years hence—especially in rivers where steelhead are not native.

I've found, over the course of the years, that many Department of Natural Resources people in my state, and others, know of steelhead rivers but they often keep quiet about it. I'm not sure why this is done in light of the massive numbers of steelhead fishermen. Some of these rivers, admittedly, are small and shallow and the sight of big steelhead sometimes brings out the outlaw in some people. But in larger rivers, such as the one near my home, it would behoove the Department of Natural Resources to inform people of the fact that steelhead are available in close relationship to major urban areas. This would take some of the crunch off other well-known steelhead streams.

Fishermen everywhere should make a point to try some of the unknown rivers and streams closer to home. One of those streams may be a big producer.

CHAPTER

11

Safety And Etiquette

One of my first remembrances of steelhead fishing as a boy was on a glorious sunny day in late April. The snows had melted and the runoff had already done just that. I was fishing a deep hole below a steep, slippery clay ledge. Two late spawning steelhead were working the gravel at the tail end of the pool.

As I intently fished, I heard running footsteps approach the river. A fisherman bedecked in brand new waders and fishing tackle, stormed over the hill at the edge of the river and started toward me on the run. "They tell me there are steelhead in this river!", he shouted, as he reached the water's edge.

Before I could open my mouth his right foot landed on the yellowish-grey clay, his leg shot out in front of him in a ridiculous manner, and he forthwith took a very undignified header into the middle of the river. The current caught his thrashing body and washed it deep into the large hole I'd been fishing. Of course, the steelhead took off at the first splash.

I laid my rod and reel on shore and hurried around to the shallow gravel to haul out the erstwhile fisherman as he washed up onto the knee-deep gravel. Several seconds later his hat popped to the surface and was quickly followed by a red face spitting water like a blowing whale.

I helped him to his feet and quickly noticed his brand-new rod and reel had disappeared in the bowels of the hole. His waders were full and he was sputtering about nearly drowning. Actually he was in no danger of drowning but he didn't know that. He walked back to his car muttering about what a dangerous sport steelhead fishing was.

This fisherman had made three crucial mistakes when he approached the stream. He didn't check the water to find out what hazards lay downstream from his crossing spot prior to wading, he didn't note the swiftness of the current and he didn't look at the bottom in time to spot the slippery clay ledge. Ten seconds of checking the river, before wading, would have saved this man an unnecessary spill, his tackle and his steelhead fishing enthusiasm.

Many fishermen never realize their full potential as a steelheader simply because they have not acquired a proficiency at wading. Steelhead streams range from gentle coldwater streams rarely over five feet deep, to large brawling western rivers with loose rocks and boulders underfoot. A steelhead fisherman is judged by the way he handles himself in the water. Good wading techniques take years of practice to master.

Wading for steelhead normally means chest-high waders. Hip boots or waist-high waders aren't the answer on a steelhead stream. A hooked fish will often take the fisherman downstream through deep, heavy water where the hip-boot clad fisherman would either have to break off or get wet.

Buying Waders

Most waders come with a ripple sole, which is fine for many wading situations. Quality waders can be purchased in plastic, rubber, rubberized canvas, or canvas. You can special-order bootfoot models with felt soles for slippery surfaces, and with an insulated foot for coldweather steelhead fishing.

Felt wading sandals can be purchased to fasten onto the soles of a pair of ripple-soled waders for extra safety. Some steelhead fishermen make inexpensive felts from pieces of indoor-outdoor carpeting. Contact cement will adhere the carpeting to the rubber boot foot.

Every steelhead fisherman that purchases a pair of waders should purchase a belt to cinch up tightly around his waist. The belt isn't to hold his waders up, it's to keep the water out if he should upend in the river. A quality pair of suspenders will hold the waders up under your armpits. Try your waders on in the store with at least one pair (two pair is better) of wool socks on and an amount of clothing comparable to what you'll wear wading. You should be able to stand on one foot and raise the other foot about twenty-four inches without any binding or pinching in the crotch. Feet, with heavy socks on, should be snug-fitting but not tight.

Wading Safety

Almost every steelhead fisherman worthy of the title has found himself "one step over the line" on occasion. This means he'd gotten himself into the position of not being able to turn and head back upstream to safety; the current is too strong and the sheer force of the rushing water builds up on the wader's body and literally forces him downstream. At times like this, there is great comfort in wearing a Stearns life vest or one of the carbon dioxide inflatable life preservers that inflates with a squeeze of the package.

The first thing to learn about wading is best learned before you ever enter the river. Take the time and trouble to check out the water downstream from your crossing or fishing point in case you hook a fish or for some other reason are forced to go downstream. A fisherman that doesn't know the water is in big trouble before he sets foot in the river. Check for clay ledges, sudden holes or dropoffs, silt beds, muck bottoms, etc. *before* you find yourself "one step over the line."

Once you have checked out the river and made mental notes of shoreline markings to mark hazardous spots, pick a spot to enter the river. Always try to enter the river in a shallow location. Avoid the fast, knee-deep areas; swift, powerful water is capable of throwing an inexperienced wader off balance by striking him in the knees.

Most fishermen have two feet: one foot is called the lead foot and the other is called the anchor foot. The lead foot is always moved first as you probe ahead for safe footing. Gently move small stones with your foot until you feel secure in placing your weight on that foot. The lead foot also feels for slippery clay or other things that may lead to trouble.

Once the lead foot is securely in position bring the anchor foot up behind it in a smooth sliding movement. Never try to lift the back (anchor) foot up out of the water to move it. Instead slide it slowly through the water without dragging it over the gravel. This prevents noise from the foot scrubbing gravel together.

With the anchor foot in place, transfer the weight back to it and probe ahead with the lead foot again. With just a bit of practice this maneuver can be both fast and quiet—and safe.

There is a peculiar wading problem in sandy-bottomed rivers. A fisherman wades downstream in bliss and carefully fishes every hole or run. Finally he stops at the edge of a hole rimmed with sand. As he fishes, the current swirls around his feet and washes the sand from under his feet. The next thing we know the fishermen is struggling in a vain attempt to climb back up the edge of the hole. Next step—a quick dunking. The moral here is to watch your step in sandy-bottomed rivers; they can be as dangerous as a swift whitewater stream.

Watch your body placement in the stream in relation to the flow of the current. Never completely turn your back on fast current. Always try to have one side turned toward the current. This gives the current less surface area to press against. This is particularly important when crossing the river or while working into position in midstream to lay a fly over a likely-looking steelhead spot. Progress in a crab-like across and downstream manner. Allow the current to help move you downstream as you keep your body sideways to the current and move slowly across the river. If you do it properly, you'll find yourself in the best spot to fish and you'll have approached the lie in the proper manner. Never try to wade into deep heavy water by coming directly across stream.

I see quite a few waders act as if steelhead cannot hear or pick up vibrations. I've seen steelhead spook off a spawning redd when a fisherman scuffed his feet in the gravel one hundred yards upstream. Steelhead are hard enough to catch without giving them advance warning with sloppy footwork.

Learn to pick your feet up slowly and smoothly and place them down softly but firmly. Never allow your feet to slide through the gravel. Small stones rubbing together create quite a din underwater and this sound can be transmitted a long way.

Some steelhead rivers are sandy or silt-bottomed. Small puffs of sand or silt kicked up by an over-eager wader will often drift downstream and spook the steelhead. The best alternative in many cases is to approach a hole or run from downstream where noise or disturbed sand or silt isn't a major factor.

Wading Staffs

A wading staff can be a valuable asset when wading in swift currents, deep water or rivers with large slippery stones or boulders on the bottom. A staff can be easily made from a fiberglass ski pole. A sturdy chest-high branch will suffice under most circumstances. There are many commercially made wading staffs on the market. The best ones have a hook on the end to probe for the bottom and a leather or elastic thong on the other end to hold onto.

A staff should be used as a third leg or balance point when shifting position in the current. Always use the wading staff on your upstream side. Place the point of the staff firmly on the bottom of the river for support, and then move your lead and anchor feet to position yourself. The staff can float in the water near you on the short thong when not in use.

Many western anglers use large rocks or boulders to break the flow of current in treacherous water. Select a course that will place you just downstream from a large boulder; a small pocket of eddy water will be found behind each boulder and this quiet water will allow you to rest momentarily before picking another path to another boulder. Boulder-to-boulder wading is an exceptionally easy way to navigate rough wading water.

There are certain tricks that work occasionally if you feel yourself losing your balance. The normal involuntary reaction to falling is to throw out your arms in an attempt to offset the loss of balance. A momentary loss of balance can often be countered by slamming your rod down into the water and pushing on it. The water pressure on the rod will act as a steadying hand and will sometimes prevent a dunking.

I remember a time I was following a buck steelhead down the river and tripped over a submerged log. I did a couple of half-steps trying to keep my balance. Just about the time I was ready to topple into the drink, the steelhead gave a sudden surge and the extra pull against my rod was just enough to help me regain my balance.

If you upend in a river the first thing to do is keep calm. Panic is the determining factor in drowning deaths—not trapped air in the waders. Always bear in mind that the water current, flowing downstream, will eventually push you in close to shore or onto a shallow gravel or sand bar. It doesn't pay to struggle needlessly against the current. You're wet already and the best thing to do is be sure you've got a good lungful of air at all times and try to keep track of your downstream progress. If possible, try to float downstream feet first to avoid striking your head on some unseen object in the water.

As you drift downstream try to work gradually toward the closest shore. A few strokes with your arms will often make the difference between a long ride and a short one.

Many times the fisherman will merely be able to hippety-hop through a deep hole without losing his balance. This is normally what happens when you take that one extra step over the line and can't turn and go back.

Safety Equipment

I advise every steelhead fisherman to wear a belt outside his waders and cinch it up tightly. The belt will trap air in the wader legs and this very air, when the legs are doubled up, will act as buoyant cushions and can float you right to safety. And the belt will prevent excess water from filling your wader legs. No fisherman should wade in water over his hips without having a belt tightly secured around his waist.

A Stearns Fisherman Flotation jacket is just the berries for winter steelheading. It effectively cuts the bite of a chilly breeze as well as serving as a life jacket. I've found the Stearns Pocket Vest model to be just right for warm weather steelheading.

A tip for waders—one of the finest means of patching all types of waders or hipboots is available in a tube. Dow Corning manufactures a silicone rubber Bathtub Caulk in several different colors. It dries quickly on any clean dry surface and the patch lasts for a long time.

STREAM ETIQUETTE

Etiquette is as much at home on a steelhead stream, lake or tidal basin as it is in a formal restaurant. The gist of fishing etiquette, to paraphrase the golden rule, is to treat other fishermen

A lone flyfisherman on the Clearwater in British Columbia. *(British Columbia Government photo)*

the way you'd like to be treated. Our rivers are becoming too crowded for anyone to ignore the rules of good sportsmanship and stream courtesy.

The particular rules of streamside etiquette will vary considerably from one river to another or one geological area to another. What works well on a western stream may not be necessary on a Great Lakes river.

For instance, on many of the western rivers the riverboats make a float down through a drift and fish as they go. Another boat will often follow at a discreet distance and on many of the more popular drifts, it will be an endless procession of drift boats fishing the same water throughout the day. If a fisherman wants to fish the drift again, he has to move back upstream to the head of the drift, wait his turn, and make the drift the second time. On western rivers, no one anchors in a drift and fishes the best spot. Protocol has it that no one has the right, even on an uncrowded stream, to anchor in one location.

However, on many of the larger Great Lakes streams, tradition allows that the first boat into a hole or run can anchor wherever it chooses, and fish that stretch of river as long as it cares to. Many boats will anchor in the middle of a drift at daybreak, and fish there the entire day. And woe be to anyone that has the nerve to drop in downstream from where they're fishing.

The wading fisherman needs to be more sensitive to etiquette than the boat fisherman because he's in much closer contact with his fellow fisherman. Again, regional traditions rule. Very few Great Lakes fishermen care to have someone intrude into their hole or run unless the river is so large they can't cover it adequately. Then they are expected to ask before intruding. The idea of another fisherman encroaching on a man working steelhead on a spawning bed has been known to lead to violence. It simply goes against the grain of many Great Lakes fishermen to fish elbow-to-elbow with other steelheaders. The only exception to this rule is when anglers congregate below a hydro dam which effectively blocks the upstream migration of steelhead. Here anglers congregate in large numbers, and the fishing is very productive and everyone seems to get along with his fellow fisherman. But this is only out of necessity.

In the West anglers often form "lines" down through the best drifts or runs and everyone fishes briefly in one area and then shuffles off downstream. This type of fishing gives everyone a good chance to fish the best part of the pool without anyone hogging the prime locations. If someone hooks a steelhead, nearby anglers reel their lines in until the fortunate fisherman either has his fish under control or is able to lead the fish up or downstream out of the way of other fishermen.

In the shallow Great Lakes spawning streams anglers often stalk their steelhead and fish them on redds. An innocent angler could stomp down the middle of the stream and spook every steelhead within one hundred yards. Great Lakes etiquette calls for a fisherman to silently walk the bank and skirt another angler widely, without spooking the fish he's watching. If you see a man on shore, staring at the water, he's probably watching a nervous pair of steelhead on a redd. Call out and ask if he's got fish on a bed. If the answer is affirmative, circle around him to avoid scaring his fish, and move on.

Boating Rules

There are inherent etiquette problems in trolling. The majority of steelhead trolling is done with a fairly long line—at least seventy-five to one hundred yards behind the boat. Boating manners demands that other trollers never cut directly across your stern. To do so will result in a monumental tangle, and a waste of time for both boats.

When a steelhead is hooked by another troller, it is just good manners for other nearby boats to steer clear of the battle. It's nice to watch a thrilling scrap but do so from a distance. Give the man with the fish every opportunity to land his fish.

Rules of the road apply to steelhead boats, just as to driving a car. Learn the basics of who has the right of way on river or lake when boating and everyone will have more fun.

And etiquette sometimes means offering assistance to a fisherman when he requests help. I've hooked steelhead that I haven't been able to follow due to high water conditions. At times like this I've asked for help in netting a steelhead.

But, anyone that seeks assistance in netting a fish should be prepared to lose it. I've always preferred netting my own fish whenever possible, but occasionally a fisherman must put his trust in others.

Particular problems exist on rivers where an abundance of both boat and wading traffic exist. Squabbles often develop when boats drift or motor through a hole being fished by waders, the contention being that the boat will spook feeding steelhead. I personally feel just the opposite; I believe that a drift boat or boat under power can often stir a steelhead into striking. I also believe just as strongly that the boat fisherman should do everything in his power to keep from becoming a nuisance to the wading angler. The wader, on the other hand, has to realize the boatman has an equal right to the river and his means of fishing it.

THE FUTURE

The future of steelhead fishing looks pretty secure to me. Certain isolated steelhead fisheries have taken a definite decline, but the overall picture is much rosier than for certain other species of fish.

Pollution And Dams

Nevertheless man's consuming lust for rapid growth and expansion has ruined many streams that were once grade A steelhead rivers. The preceding century brought land use practices to many portions of the West Coast and Great Lakes states that left ugly scars still visible today. Entire watersheds were timbered off and left nude to erode during winter rains. Shallow spawning bars were stripped of fine gravel for highway fill. Tons of insecticides sprayed on crops were later washed into ditches, which emptied into streams which ultimately fed the chemicals into the Pacific Ocean or one of the Great Lakes.

In the West, rapid expansion created a heavy demand for power, and hydro dams sprouted on western streams like dandelions on a spring lawn. The dams were cited as providing needed power, giving additional employment to areas badly in need of jobs. But no one foresaw the devastation they could wreak on age-old steelhead spawning grounds.

The influence dams have had on steelheading cannot be measured. The steelhead runs that once filled Idaho's Salmon and Clearwater river systems are now a trickle; no one knows whether they are capable of coming back or not. Towering dams on the Columbia River have impeded the migration of fish into the Idaho drainage.

Nitrogen saturation below the dams is another deadly menace to steelhead. The super-saturated water causes steelhead to suffer symptoms similar to the "bends" that divers get. This effect kills many steelhead yearly.

The Great Lakes were recently found to have high DDT levels. This hard pesticide was formerly sprayed on fruit trees and in other areas to combat insects. Everytime it rained, DDT washed downstream and into the lakes. Steelhead, salmon and lake trout were found to have high concentrations of the chemical in their flesh. A ban was placed on the sale and use of the pesticide several years ago and the levels have slowly dropped to a safer point.

But now these large inland seas are now faced with another pollutant: PCB (polychlorinated biphenyls). This group of compounds is used in a diverse number of industrial compounds and processes. Some of the largest uses are fire-resistant hydraulic fluids, heat transfer fluids, plasticizers and specialty inks in certain paper products. Although PCB pollution is heaviest in lake trout and chubs, the potential health hazard is certainly present to any human ingesting a reasonably steady diet of steelhead. A ban on the sale and use of polychlorinated biphenyls is of paramount importance to everyone, not only fishermen.

Pollution takes many forms. Although littering doesn't seem nearly as serious as PCB or DDT, it still casts a black eye on many streams.

I have special permission to fish certain sections of river flowing through private property simply because the landowner once saw me walking down the river bank with a net full of trash. "Them all your beer cans?" he asked, nodding to the case of empty cans in my net. "Nope, don't drink beer. I pick up cans though." I've been free to fish his property ever since.

Indian Claims

Another larger and more difficult problem is facing steelhead and the sport of steelhead fishing: legal precedents making it legal for Indians in the West and Midwest to harvest steelhead by any means.

I'm not anti-Indian. But I am against anything that is injurious to the good of the majority of the fishermen and steelhead. And there is a definite movement afoot in the courts to give people of Indian descent unlimited fishing privileges at the expense of the rights of the majority of citizens.

Sunset falls over a rivermouth fisherman in the Great Lakes. *(Photo by the author)*

The argument goes that Indians have been denied certain treaty rights offered by the U.S. Government many years ago. Modern-day interpretation of these rights certainly does not give an Indian the right to use commercial gill nets, sonar equipment, gill net tugs, and other specialized gear that were not in existence at the time of the treaty.

Few fishermen would argue the fact Indians are entitled to enough fish for immediate table use. But the modern Indians' demands go far beyond that point; they feel fish must be made available for Indians to harvest in any manner. To compound this travesty, people having only a smallest trace of Indian blood are now claiming Indian treaty privileges.

Commercial Fisheries

Oregon now has a law which prohibits the purchase or sale of steelhead, and manages steelhead and other rainbow trout for recreational angling. Just a couple of years ago it was legal to buy and sell steelhead in Oregon. Unfortunately, netting with sophisticated gill nets has been legal in the Columbia River for years. Nearly one thousand gill netters rake the mighty Columbia River with miles of nylon. Approximately half this number are from Oregon and the other half are Washington residents. Reports show that enough gill netters are present on the Columbia River to take approximately eighty percent of the trout and salmon from a stretch of river within seven days. This is an astronomical figure. Many of these steelhead were destined to provide sport for millions of fishermen in Oregon, Washington and Idaho.

It does little good for a state to stock steelhead from hatcheries and have wild native fish contributing to the carrying capacity of the stream if gill netters are free to net the fish in open water or as they migrate upstream. The first and most vital point is the resource must be managed for the benefit of the greatest number of people and for the best interests of the fish. I've researched several states which have both steelhead and gill netters and the commercial fishermen always number less than 500 per state. Some states have only one hundred or fewer commercial fishermen. It's a fact that sportfishermen are many times more numerous than commercial fishermen.

Michigan has rid its portion of the Great Lakes of commercial fishing. The oldtime gill netters have been bought out by the state and gill netting is becoming a thing of the past. There is still a large amount of illegal gill netting by Indians in certain areas, a problem we'll likely have until the Supreme Court settles the case of Indian treaty rights.

Beyond these serious and immediate problems, steelhead fishing stands on a pretty solid foundation and the overall outlook is bright. But steelhead fishermen must realize that continued good fishing is something they must fight for. If every steelhead fisherman joins an active steelhead club, represents his area by joining forces with fisheries people, learns as much as possible about future programs, and makes his influence felt on legislators, steelhead fishing can do nothing but improve.

Index